Army of Worn Soles

Scott Bury

Army of Worn Soles

Cover design by David C. Cassidy

Edited by Rebecca Tsaros Dickson

Quality control by iAi Independent Authors International

Published by The Written Word Communications Company, Ottawa, Ontario, Canada

www.writtenword.ca

ISBN 978-0-9879141-9-4

Library and Archives Canada Cataloguing in Publication information is available.

Army of Worn Soles

IN MEMORY OF MAURICE BURY

Dedicated to Roxanne

CONTENTS

THANK YOU

Thanks to Rebecca Tsaros Dickson, Frederick Lee Brooke, Alan McDermott, Elise Stokes and David C. Cassidy for invaluable advice. And thanks especially to David Cassidy for an outstanding cover.

And of course, thanks to my family, Roxanne, Evan and Nicolas for your support and tolerance of a man obsessed with writing down a story.

Chapter 1: Prisoner of War

Kharkiv, October 1941

Maurice put the bottle on the ground beside him and took off his uniform shirt. He spread it on the smoothest piece of ground he could find, then laid the bottle near the officer's insignia on the collar and pushed down. He rolled the bottle over tattered, light-brown material until the lice cracked under the glass. Back and forth, twice, three times. He felt a dull satisfaction at his first pathetic victory in more than half a year.

The effort was exhausting. His stomach ached and his throat burned with thirst.

He slumped back until he leaned against the barracks. Men in grey uniforms stood or walked across the cobbled courtyard of the ancient castle. One came toward him, a slim man with light brown hair and hazel eyes. He stopped in front of Maurice and leaned down.

"Maurice? Is it you?"

Breathing required effort. So did looking up. Maurice had not eaten in days, but he still trusted his sight. He knew the man with the light-brown hair and hazel eyes, even in a Wehrmacht uniform.

"Maurice?" the young man said again. "What are you

doing here?"

He couldn't swallow. His mouth held no moisture. "Dying. I'm starving to death." Maurice closed his eyes and hung his head.

Bohdan crouched beside him. "You got drafted?"

Maurice made the effort to look up at his old friend. "The Red Army made me a lieutenant. What the hell are you doing here and in a German uniform, Bohdan?"

"The Germans kicked the Russians out, something we couldn't do. Why shouldn't I join the winning side? And it's 'Daniel' now, not Bohdan." He looked around to make sure no one noticed him, a Wehrmacht officer, talking to a prisoner of war. "I'm glad you survived, that you were captured instead of killed. The Germans killed a lot of Red soldiers."

"I know. I was there."

Bohdan looked around again. "How did you get here?"

"Like you said, we were captured, the whole army, outside Kharkiv. They brought us here."

Bohdan shook his head. "Are you all right? I'll see if I can bring you anything, but I have to be careful."

Maurice looked into his friend's eyes. "Get me out of here."

"Set a prisoner free? Are you crazy?"

"Bohdan—sorry, Daniel, you're my best friend. Or you were. If I ever meant anything to you, get me out."

Daniel-Bohdan looked left and right again. "I cannot let Red soldiers go," he whispered.

Maurice took a dry breath. His strength was almost gone. "You're an officer in a victorious army. You have the power. You can get me out, me and my boys.

Daniel shook his head and stood. "Stalin's going to surrender within six months, and then all the prisoners will be freed. Hitler has promised freedom for all nations. We'll all be free. Ukraine will be free."

Maurice looked at the ground between his splayed legs.

He could no longer lift his head. "I can't wait six months. I can't wait two days. If you wait, you'll find a corpse. We'll all be dead. You have to get us out now."

Daniel hesitated. He looked around the camp again, but no one paid attention. "So the Reds made you an officer, did they? Where are your men? All dead?"

Somewhere, Maurice found the strength to stand up again. He staggered to the barracks door, went in and called his *odalenye*, the unit he commanded. "Step over here, boys."

Daniel followed Maurice inside, and Maurice wondered if Daniel wasn't breaking some regulation by entering prisoners' quarters unaccompanied by at least one guard.

Daniel scanned the room, taking in the defeated, injured and starving men. No one threatened him. They did not even move. Maurice realized when they saw Daniel, they saw their captor.

Daniel stepped out of the barracks and waited outside the door. "I'll see what I can do, Maurice. But you're on the wrong fucking side."

Maurice picked up the bottle and returned to crushing the lice out of his uniform shirt. It was the only thing he could do to reduce his misery.

He thought about the last time he had seen Bohdan, before he became Daniel.

It was in the gymnasium, the pre-university school in Peremyshl. What used to be Poland. What a long, strange, twisted path my life has followed.

Chapter 2: Gymnasium

Peremyshl, Poland, 1937

Maurice sat on the front steps and opened his chemistry textbook on his lap. He scratched his jaw, looked across the street, down at his feet and up again, unconsciously drumming his fingers on the concrete steps.

Concentrate, he reminded himself. He focused on the page and willed himself to learn the words and concepts. His left foot tap-tapped on the step. His mouth felt dry, but he resisted the urge to get a drink of water.

"You want a cigarette?"

Maurice looked up at a thin man his own age, with light brown hair and hazel eyes. He held a pack of cigarettes toward Maurice. "You look like you need one."

Maurice drew one from the pack. "Thanks," he said, and dug matches out of his pocket.

The young man shook a cigarette loose for himself and let Maurice light it, then sat on the step beside him. "I'm Bohdan." He held out his hand.

"I'm Maurice. Where are you from?"

"Here. Peremyshl. You?"

"Nastaciv. A little village near Ternopyl."

"You nervous about Brother Michael's chemistry class? I don't blame you. The Brother is a tough bastard."

"Chemistry is not my strongest subject. Neither is math. I'm better with languages."

"Is that so? I'm the opposite. I can't keep Latin tenses straight. What languages do you speak?"

"Polish, Russian, English. A little German, and I hope to learn more German here."

"And Ukrainian, of course," Bohdan said, smiling.

Maurice laughed. He took a final drag on the cigarette and then took a package of biscuits from his canvas school bag. "Here, these just arrived from my mother in the mail. She must have sent them the same day I got on the train to come here."

Bohdan squashed his cigarette under his shoe, smiled again and took a biscuit. "These are very good."

"Yes. I could live on these biscuits." Maurice popped one into his mouth.

"Where did you learn English?" Bohdan asked.

"I was born in Montreal."

"Canada?" Bohdan whistled. "Interesting. Usually people emigrate the other way, from Europe to America."

"My parents did, of course. My father has a business in Montreal, washing windows in big buildings. But with the Depression, business is slow, so my mother decided to return to the farm until my father can build up the business again. He's been to visit us a few times."

"So you're back in Poland. Think it was the right choice?"

Maurice shrugged. "I guess so. We always have enough to eat. The farm does all right. It's a lot of work, but..."

Bohdan leaned closer and spoke softly to be certain no one else could overhear. "But in Canada, you were free."

Maurice spoke low, too. "And here, we're not even allowed to speak our own language."

The two young men were quiet for a while, looking in different directions without seeing the city in front of them. Maurice broke the silence. "Languages are important, but it seems some are more important than others. Latin, Greek—those are most important to the teachers and priests who run this school. I'm good at those. How good are you with chemistry and sciences?"

"I got *A*s last year," Bohdan said. "All right. You help me with Latin and Greek, and I'll help you with math and Brother Michael's chemistry assignments. All right?"

Maurice held out his hand. "It's a deal."

World War II moved international borders. In 1937, a large section of Western Galicia, what the Ukrainians called Halychyna, lay within Poland. The Polish government tried to suppress Ukrainian culture, even going so far as to ban the use of the Ukrainian language in public. The Ukrainian Gymnasia managed to use its Catholic Church affiliation to defy the government and offer secondary and post-secondary education in Ukrainian. They became bastions of Ukrainian culture in Halychyna.

Staffed by Ukrainian priests and brothers, the gymnasia offered a classical education, stressing Latin, Greek, philosophy and history with a little science, bridging the gap between a sporadic primary education and university. Maurice settled in quickly and impressed the teachers with his ability in languages and history, but struggled with mathematics.

On a Friday afternoon in September, Maurice and Bohdan sat in an otherwise empty classroom as the light outside the windows failed. Maurice struggled to grasp a finer point of trigonometry, and Bohdan struggled not to show his frustration. After a half-hour on a single problem, Maurice pretended to understand. "So, this ratio is the same as that one?"

"Yes, exactly. You've got it."

Maurice didn't feel like he had anything, but he could remember the steps needed to find the sine of one angle given the shape of a triangle on the far side of a complex drawing. He closed his books. "Good. Thanks. I think that's enough for tonight."

They went out into the soft September evening and lit cigarettes. "So, Maurice, are you interested in making a little money?" Bohdan asked as they walked to the corner, blowing smoke into the darkening sky.

"Sure, but how?"

"I know some Jewish families who will pay to have their firewood chopped for them. It's hard work, but it'll put cigarette money in your pocket."

"I have a free morning tomorrow."

"Good. Do you think anyone else in the dormitory would like to come along?"

"How many do you need?"

"Four boys make a good team, so ask two more."

The next day, Maurice knocked on the back door of Bohdan's parents' house. Behind him stood two young men from the dormitory. Yvan was small and thin with stringy blond hair, and was beginning to develop a reputation for practical jokes. Michael was a little taller than Maurice, skinny with black hair and dark eyes. He struggled in practically every class, but he was always willing to take part in anything.

Bohdan, wearing overalls and sturdy boots, handed each of the other three a pair of work gloves. "Let's go," he said.

Within an hour, all four boys were sweating in the back garden of a large brick house in the Jewish quarter. Maurice and Bohdan each had one end of a double-handled saw, moving in tandem to cut logs into one-foot lengths. Michael split the logs into four sections each, and Yvan split half of those into kindling. After another hour, they had a respectable stack of wood and another of kindling along the back wall of the house. A stout, middle-aged maid came out of the back door, nodded in satisfaction and dropped a few coins into each of their outstretched hands, then told them to come back next week.

"A few *zloty*, but it's enough to buy cigarettes for a week," Michael said.

"Come on, boys, we've time to cut wood for two more Jews before the day is done," Bohdan said, and led them down the street to another substantial house.

By the end of the day, they were all exhausted, covered in sweat and sawdust. But they felt wealthy enough to buy their supper and a bottle of beer at a cafe. When he got back to the dormitory in the early evening, Maurice dropped heavily onto his cot and fell asleep immediately.

In the morning, Maurice counted the coins and few banknotes he had earned the day before—almost ten zlotys. A generous amount of pocket money for the week, but it wouldn't make a difference when it came to paying tuition. And it wasn't enough to compensate for the whole day of sweating, the ache in his shoulders, or the rawness of his hands.

The next week, when the boys went to the Jewish quarter, Maurice stepped in front of Bohdan and knocked on the kitchen door. A man dressed all in black answered. He had a long grey beard, spectacles and a cap on his head. "Good morning, sir," Maurice said. Warm air filled with delicious aromas came out of the kitchen. "We're here to cut your firewood."

The man nodded, frowning. His eyes scanned Maurice and his friends, and the pile of uncut wood beside the garden. He didn't say anything, so Maurice pulled off his cap and smiled as warmly as he could. He held out his hand. "I am Maurice, and these are my friends. We did a good job last week, wouldn't you say."

The homeowner nodded without smiling, but he shook Maurice's hand. "Yes, fine. Go to it, then."

"Yes, sir, we will, right away, but there is just one thing," Maurice said. He heard his friends shuffling behind him, mystified as to what he was doing. "Last week, you paid us fifty *grozy*, just half a zloty each to cut and stack your firewood and make kindling, too. And believe me, we are grateful—hmm, my, that smells good in your kitchen—grateful for the work. But you see, your honour, we are students at the gymnasium. Ukrainians, underdogs like your people. And the food at the gymnasium is not as good as the food in your kitchen. Are you baking?"

"What do you want?"

"Mister—I am sorry, I don't know your name?"

"Kohn."

"Mr. Kohn, rabbi—"

"I am not a rabbi, I am a printer."

"My apologies. Please, sir, Mr. Kohn—we are four poor Ukrainian students, struggling to improve our lives and our families', too. My mother, for instance, lives on a poor farm near Ternopyl, and my education is a great burden on her. Just think of how hard she had to work to pay the tuition, let alone my living expenses. And my friends are in the same situation." He indicated the three boys behind him.

Kohn sighed deeply. "What do you want?"

"A zloty each."

"A zloty. I can get any *goy* for a fraction of that. Go on."

"Hear me out, Mr. Kohn. One zloty for each of us will allow us to buy a good supper tonight, and we are all hard-working boys, and we'll send money home to our mothers. And in return, we'll cut twice as much wood as last week—"

"I don't need twice as much wood. I still haven't burned all the wood you cut last week."

"Maybe. But you could sell some of your surplus to other households."

"So I'm supposed to peddle cut wood to my neighbours?"

Maurice had not anticipated that response.

Bohdan stepped forward. "Of course not. We'll sell it and give you the proceeds."

Mr. Kohn shook his head. "You *goyim* have no head for

money. This is how it will work, boys. Instead of fifty grozy each, I'll pay you twenty-five. You cut as much wood for me as you did last week. Then you cut as much as you like to sell to the Abrahams next door—Abraham never buys enough wood, the cheapskate. You charge him five zlotys for the week. That way you'll have more money than you did before. And you come back here and give me a quarter of what he paid, and I'll let you come back next week. I'll have more wood for you to sell then."

Maurice turned to the others, who nodded. It was a good deal if it meant more work for each of them.

Kohn dug in a front pocket and pulled out some coins. "Here are another twenty-five grozy for each of you—buy yourselves a beer after. And never let it be said that Chaim Kohn let anyone, even goyim, go hungry." He closed the door.

The boys got to work, spending the whole morning and part of the afternoon cutting two weeks' worth of firewood. They stacked Kohn's up against the wall, and the rest on a sledge. They were about to drag it next door when the kitchen door opened again and a young blond maid stepped out, carrying a tray piled with bread, cups, a kettle and a large jar of pickles.

"Mr. Kohn says you boys must have worked up an appetite," she said in Ukrainian.

Maurice realized he was famished. The boys stuffed bread into their mouths and sipped the tea carefully.

The maid was pretty, and could not have been more than eighteen years old. But before he could say anything, Bohdan put his cup down and stepped closer to her. "Have you been working for the Jews for long, dear?"

She gave him a sceptical look. "Long enough to know not to be charmed by poor students covered in sweat and sawdust. Now finish your tea and take the wood to the Abrahams next door. They're expecting you."

Although Abraham expected them, he was unhappy about buying Kohn's surplus, but too embarrassed to appear cheaper than Kohn to turn them down. "Bigshot Kohn thinks he's doing me such a favour," he muttered, as he gave Maurice a five-zloty note.

The afternoon was wearing as they went to the next house they had visited the week before. Maurice repeated the deal they had worked out with Kohn. The man of the house, Weiss, conferred with his wife about the idea and nodded.

At the end of the day, they had cut a little more wood than the week before. Their shoulders and backs ached, their palms were callused, but they had ten zloty more.

"You're quite a charmer with the Jews," Bohdan said, slapping Maurice's aching back as they stuffed themselves with cabbage rolls at a diner in the Ukrainian sector of the city. "Be careful, buddy—if Kohn finds out you know how to make money, he'll marry you to his daughter."

Maurice nearly choked on his tea. In ethnically divided eastern Poland in 1937, even the thought of marrying a Jewish girl felt foreign and dangerous.

With the work they did cutting and selling firewood, Maurice and his friends had a few coins in their pockets. And for Maurice, he was able to write his mother, telling her he didn't need as much money every month.

Mail was always a cause for celebration. The students' parents would send packages with news from home, knitted sweaters and socks, cakes and cookies and other food that would survive a trip through the mail. The students would gather to share and swap their goodies and exchange news about parents and sisters and nephews.

Slawko, a heavyset teen, was the son of Father Ihor, one of the Ukrainian Catholic priests that taught at the gymnasium and the one in charge of student discipline. He never brought treats from home. At night, he would look at the boys snacking on their mamas' goodie packages, his face long, chin in his hand. "I didn't get nothin'," he'd always say, and sigh until someone gave him a cookie or an apple. "How can they expect us to work all day without feeding us enough," he would whine, dropping crumbs onto his lap. Whenever another student opened his goodie packages, Slawko would always be nearby saying, "That looks good. Give me a cookie."

The students gladly shared cookies, cakes and fruit at first. But after a few weeks, they were sick of Slawko the Mooch. He never had his own treats or desserts. He never offered a younger student help with schoolwork, either. "Not that he'd be any help—he's such a blockhead," Bohdan said.

Slawko's cot was on the first floor of the dormitory, but he seemed to prefer the food from the boys on the second storey. Or maybe the boys in his own section were more tired of feeding the mooch. Whatever the reason, by the end of the first month at the gymnasium, Slawko lingered on the second storey as late as he could every evening until bed-check.

Some of the boys worked out a system to feed Slawko without having to see his mournful face or listen to his whining. Each night, every student who had received goodies that day donated something to a basket. After lights-out, the boys lowered it on a rope out the window to the eager Slawko, standing by a first-floor window. Maurice and other students would watch him snatch blindly at the basket's contents even before he took it in the window.

This system continued for weeks, until the boys tired of giving up their treats from home. One winter night after lights-out, Maurice and the other students crowded near the second-storey window, trying hard not to make noise.

Bohdan and Yvan stood beside the window, stifling their laughter. Bohdan held Slawko's basket. "Shh. Quiet, you idiots." Bohdan hissed until he was satisfied he had everyone's attention. "We're going to give old Slawko a real treat."

Yvan, who had developed a reputation as a practical

joker, could not stop giggling as he pulled a bucket from under his bed. He lifted a metal plate off the top, filling the dorm with the rich odour of horse manure. "I took it from the stable this afternoon," he said, laughing so hard, he had to put his hand over his mouth.

Oh no, Maurice thought, but he could not help feeling a wicked glee.

Yvan and Bohdan carefully dumped the manure into the basket for Slawko. They covered it with the metal plate again to keep the smell in, and then covered the whole thing with a little embroidered towel from someone's mother. The conspirators lowered the basket more carefully than usual, while Maurice and the rest crowded round the window to watch, barely able to suppress their laughter. There was much shushing as giggles escaped.

When the basket reached the lower window, a hand reached out to lift the towel. It hesitated when it touched the plate. One of the boys on the second floor could not help laughing.

The mooch lifted the metal plate and his other hand reached out and plunged into the basket.

"What the hell is this?" A voice rang out across the courtyard, echoing off the far side of the gymnasium building. "*Shit.*"

Bohdan fell back from the window onto his knees, laughing so hard that tears ran down his cheeks. Yvan nearly toppled out the window, saved only when another student grabbed his arm. Others were literally rolling on the floor.

They could hear Slawko cursing them out the window, and then loud footsteps as one of the friars on night duty came to check on the noise. Yvan tossed the bucket out the window, where it clattered loudly on the gravel. Everyone jumped into their beds and pulled their covers over themselves before the door burst open. Two brothers came in, scowling, but all they saw were apparently sleeping students.

Meanwhile, they heard another friar enter the dorm below. "What are you doing at the window? What's in that basket? *Shit*."

At that, every boy upstairs burst into laughter.

"What's going on here?" one of the night watchmen said. But from downstairs, they heard more voices. "You're right, it's shit."

One of the friars went to the open window. "Why is this window open in the winter?" He leaned out. "What's going on down there?"

"Shit. A whole picnic basket of shit," another said, and then the friar had to wait an entire minute while his counterpart downstairs laughed. "Apparently, Slawko's friends sent him a gift. It's all over his hands..." And the voice disintegrated into laughter again.

The friars upstairs were laughing, too. They closed the window, gave warning glares to all the boys in the dorm and left, shaking their heads.

The friars made Slawko clean up the mess downstairs, and wash the bucket in the courtyard. The next morning, he had to clean the latrines as punishment for being up past curfew. He scowled at the boys from the second-storey dorm, especially at Yvan and Bohdan. He could not have known who was responsible, but he had strong suspicions.

And he never begged for treats again.

Chapter 3: Drafted

Nastaciv, Ukraine, 1941

Maurice achieved high marks in languages and history, and with Bohdan's help, he achieved Bs in mathematics and science. But attending the gymnasium required money for tuition and living expenses. In Poland in the late 1930s, money was becoming more and more difficult to come by.

In August 1939, the Soviet Union and Nazi Germany signed the Molotov-von Ribbentrop Pact. In September, Germany invaded Poland and seized half of it—including Peremyshyl on both sides of the San River, the border agreed by the two powers.

With his school now in occupied territory, Maurice stayed on his mother's farm in Nastaciv. Two weeks later, Stalin ordered the Red Army to move west and seized the eastern half of the country. The USSR then invaded Finland in the Winter War, seizing and holding provinces in Karelia and, after that, annexed the Baltic states of Estonia, Latvia and Lithuania.

Lwow became Lvov and, along with the Ternopyl district, became part of the nominally autonomous Ukrainian Soviet Socialist Republic. The Soviets, ironically, relaxed the Polish restrictions on Ukrainian education, but arrested Ukrainian intellectuals and journalists.

In 1940, by virtue of his two years of education in the gymnasium, Maurice got a job as a teacher in the in Ternopyl, a school funded by parents.

One March day in 1941, Maurice came home to find his mother and sister sitting at the kitchen table, crying. "Oh, Maurice," was all his sister Hanya could say, as she pushed an envelope toward him. It had been opened, even though it was addressed to him. A Soviet government seal was on the corner. Hands shaking, Maurice pulled out the single sheet. The top of the letter read "Red Army" in black letters.

"They're ordering me to report for duty," Maurice said, his voice croaking.

"Oh, Maurice, oh dear," his mother said. "Oh, they're taking you to war."

Maurice sat and took his mother's hand in his own. "Don't worry, Mama," he said. "I don't have to fight for Russia." They all knew he was lying. "I'm a Canadian citizen."

His mother searched his face for hope. "Do you really think so?"

"Of course," he said, struggling to keep the tremble out of his voice.

Hanya and their mother, Tekla Kuritsa allowed themselves to be comforted, or at least calmed. They spent a morose evening. Maurice read newspapers, Hanya fussed around the kitchen and Tekla sat staring out the window long after dark.

The next morning was a dull March day. A damp wind chilled Maurice under his coat as he walked through the slush to the armoury in Ternopyl. A few young men, dressed in their warmest cloths and carrying suitcases or bags, waited nervously at the gate. No one spoke.

One by one, they gave their draft notices to a man in the greenish-brown uniform of the Red Army, sitting behind a table. The officer, a young Russian with a broad face and deep brown eyes, asked each inductee's name, checked it off a list, examined the draft letter and gave the man another piece of paper. Then he sent him to wait in another room, where each inductee would be loaded onto a train and sent to a training camp.

Some of the men tried to tell the officer why they shouldn't be inducted: they were needed at their jobs, at home, they were essential workers, they weren't healthy. The officer first told each who addressed him in his native Ukrainian to speak Russian. Then he dismissed each argument with, "The Motherland needs you, tovarisch. Report back here tomorrow ready to ship out or you'll be arrested."

Maurice felt sure he had a better argument than the man in front of him, who said his employer, a machine shop, absolutely could not do without him. "Wonderful, comrade," the officer said. "The army needs skilled machinists like you. You will ship out today." The shocked machinist sputtered incoherently as a soldier took his arm and led him to join the other recruits at the train station.

Maurice stepped to the table. "Good morning, sir. I know you're busy, so I would like to quickly help you resolve an error—my draft letter is a mistake." He put it on the table in front of the officer.

The officer looked up, arching one eyebrow. "That's a new one. What kind of mistake?"

"I am not eligible for service, as I am not a citizen of the Soviet Union. I'm a Canadian." He showed his birth certificate.

The officer struggled to sound out the Roman lettering. "Doh-meen-i-yon off Kanada," he read. He frowned, then shook his head and looked Maurice straight in the eyes. "You are still required to report for duty, comrade."

"But I'm a Canadian citizen."

"It doesn't matter, tovarisch. You live here now and you must help defend the Motherland." He was already looking at the next man in line. "Report to the train station by seven tomorrow morning or you'll be arrested. Next."

Maurice's flash of anger was quickly replaced by a despairing acceptance. He had known all along the Soviet army would never care about such an insignificant detail as his citizenship.

He took the long way home, stopping in a café for hot tea as much for the warmth as to delay telling his family the bad news.

He returned to the little farm by lunchtime. Tekla and Hanya wept quietly when they heard. His mother even helped him pack warm clothes and tried to hold out some hope.

"Maybe there won't be a war. Maybe you'll serve your two years and then they'll let you out, and then we can all go back to Canada."

"Who would we go to war with, anyway?" Hanya asked, joining in. "Russia and Germany are allies, now. Germany is fighting England, and they're too far from us." She did not mention what they all thought: Finland remained a dreaded enemy.

"That's right," Tekla said. "Germany is our ally. There's no reason for Russia to fight them."

Maurice agreed, and they sat down to a subdued supper. Tekla poured too much of her home-made vodka, and Maurice drank it all.

The next morning, the women drove Maurice to the train station in the horse-cart. His mother gave him a big basket of food for the journey east: sausage, bread, a small flask of hot tea, some apples left from the fall, a jar of preserves.

The train station was surrounded by military policemen carrying rifles. Maurice also saw other men in peaked caps with maroon bands—the NKVD, the Soviet security police. They strutted, ordering people around in rough and guttural Russian, smoking and looking officious.

The platform was crowded with young men and their families saying goodbye. Like Hanya and Tekla, all the inductees' parents fussed over them. Mothers wept, fathers gave their sons brave smiles and manly kisses on each cheek.

Maurice thought of his father in Canada and wondered whether he worried about his family in Russian-dominated Ukraine.

"Write to us as soon as you're settled and tell us where you are and how you're doing. Please don't forget, my dear," Tekla said. She tucked his scarf closer around his neck. She had to stand on her toes to kiss his cheek. She cried, but Hanya smiled bravely.

"Be careful, Maurice. Look after yourself."

The train rumbled and squealed into the station. MPs pushed the young men onto the cars. Maurice found a seat with three fresh-faced, silent young men, all holding baskets from their mothers, looking at him as if seeking some kind of hope or comfort.

Maurice waved at his mother and sister through the window as the train chuffed away. He felt lonelier than ever before. He patted a secret pocket he had sewn under the waist of his pants, inaccessible from the outside, which held his Canadian birth certificate.

He made himself a promise: he would never part with it until he got back to Montreal.

The train stopped frequently as it rumbled east. At first, Maurice and the three men in the group of four seats just looked out the window or down at the floor. The morning wore on. Maurice wished for a cup of tea.

In mid-morning, the boy sitting across from Maurice opened the basket on his lap, letting out a delicious smell.

"What's that?" the young man beside Maurice asked. He was a thin boy with a mess of curly dark hair. The cuffs of his jacket were badly frayed.

The slightly fat, fair boy across from him pulled out a package wrapped in paper. "Meat pie. My mama makes the best meat pies around."

"Smells great," Curly said. The chubby boy unwrapped the meat pie, carefully broke off a piece and gave it to him. Curly popped it in his mouth. "Mmm. It is good." He wiped his mouth on his frayed sleeve and pulled out a jar of pickles from his own basket. "These are from my auntie." He handed one to Chubby, then offered Maurice and the fourth boy pickles. They gratefully accepted and opened their own baskets. Maurice took out some black bread and a piece of kielbasa, cut off three pieces of the sausage and handed them out to the group.

The man directly across from Maurice, who was thin and appeared to be in his mid-thirties, looked over his shoulder, checking for commissars. He took out a bottle of dark liquid and passed it to Maurice. "*Samohanka*," he whispered and took a bit of Maurice's mother's kielbasa.

Maurice took a swig of the home-brewed whisky. It was strong but he swallowed it without choking. It burned all the way down. "Thanks." He passed it to Curly.

"I'm Fedya," the thin man with the samohanka said.

Curly swigged the whiskey and passed the bottle to the chubby boy. "Thanks. I'm Borys." He then passed around some cheese.

The chubby boy choked on the whiskey and passed the bottle back to Fedya. "My name's Peter."

Maurice looked around. All over the car, young men were sharing food and drinks. A guard even took a swig of whiskey from someone near the door, then chased it down with homemade bread.

Through the morning, the train stopped at towns and villages and more inductees and guards boarded. By noon, the cars were full and young men sat on the floors or on their suitcases. Nearly everyone had a basket and traded their mother's food and their father's whiskey or vodka with each other and the guards. By midafternoon, the whole train was quietly tipsy.

Maurice dozed, waking each time the train stopped at a station or inexplicably between them, then dozed again until the train started. When sunrise streamed in through the dirty windows, Maurice was stiff and slightly hung over.

The train chuffed into another station and the guards let the men out to stretch and relieve themselves. There was no town or village near the station. The Ukrainian prairie stretched endlessly all around. Maurice thought about running, but NKVD guards with ready rifles surrounded them.

Maurice joined the line at the latrine, which was just a trough behind a wall. A commissar kept barking at them to hurry, and then, wiping their hands on their pants, they got back on the train. Through some kind of unspoken etiquette, each man found the same spot on the train, although Fedya offered his seat to a young man, a boy really, who had been squatting in a corner all night long.

The train squealed and puffed and pulled out of the station. There were no more stops at stations; every car was overflowing with young men who spoke rarely. By the end of the day, everyone's mother's food had been eaten, and their homemade liquor drunk.

On the third morning, the train pulled into a large station in a substantial town. A battered sign over the platform read "Sumy." Maurice knew it as a town in the far eastern part of Ukraine, which had been under Russia's domination for centuries.

Before the train stopped, the NKVD guards moved through the cars, poking sleeping men awake and pulling sitting men to their feet. Commissars yelled at them to get off the train, quickly.

Maurice closed his coat, patting the hidden pocket with his Canadian birth certificate. Clutching his suitcase and basket, blinking in the watery March sunlight, he followed the crowd as it moved across the station. The guards herded the men across the platform, split them into groups and pushed them aboard a succession of smaller trains. Within another hour, Maurice was marching with about a hundred other young men. They slogged down a muddy road, past a sign identifying the town of Okhtyrka, and finally into a fenced area with guards at the gates.

A commissar ordered them to line up beside the gate. A chill, damp wind made everyone shiver, although they tried hard to hide it. "All those with any secondary or post-secondary education, two steps forward," the commissar said in Russian. Maurice and a dozen or so others complied.

Are they going to shoot us as intellectuals? he wondered.

"Over that way," the commissar yelled. Maurice picked up his bags and shuffled to the right, where another commissar waited.

"Your education means you qualify for officer's training," he said. "Consider yourselves lucky. But get rid of any idea this will mean a lighter workload for you. You'll get the same basic training as every soldier. Any failure will mean you get demoted back to the enlisted ranks, with less pay, poor uniforms and no privileges. Let's go. Shut up," he said to one man who had opened his mouth to ask a question.

Two hours later, Maurice had to admit the Red Army was efficient at some things. They quickly relieved him of most of his personal belongings, putting them "in storage." He barely rescued his birth certificate from his pocket, folding it and holding it gingerly in his mouth during the group shower.

As he pulled on his new uniform, he glanced around at his fellow cadets. They looked nearly identical—young men with shaved heads, wearing the same unadorned brown tunic with turned-down collars, a leather belt over the right shoulder and across the chest to join another belt around the waist, pants baggy at the thighs, shiny, high black boots. They donned dark green caps with crimson band and piping and a black visor. Pinned to each one was a metal red star with the hammer and sickle device. Despite his feelings about being forced into the Soviet army, Maurice thought the uniform looked sharp. Except for the baby shit brown colour.

The fifty cadets were herded into a room. As they milled around, too scared to talk, yet another commissar came in and sat in the only chair in the room. He was a fat, old communist with few teeth. In a wheezy voice, he began lecturing the boys about duty and the glorious future of the workers' and peasants' state, punctuating his statements with coughs and gargling sounds. At one point, he stood, opened the door and spat outside, then returned to continue about the need to protect the state against the imperialist capitalists from Britain and America.

"We must be vigilant," he said, wheezing, then choked and coughed again. "…against espionage and propaganda inside the country, even inside the army."

A five-minute coughing fit interrupted his lecture. Some of the cadets looked alarmed, and Maurice wondered whether the old communist would die in front of them. Eventually, he gained control and resumed his lecture, telling them how the pact between the Soviet Union and the German Reich had allowed the People's Revolution to liberate the Baltic states of Estonia, Latvia and Lithuania, and to unite the Ukrainian people into a single republic.

The old man paused, coughed some more, then launched into a lecture about how each officer cadet would be trained in leading soldiers, as well as in the use of weapons so they could train the younger officers and enlisted men in their turn. "And most important," the commissar said with a lisp past his bare gums, "you will learn how important it is for you, as officers in the People's armed forces, to set an example of how communism will enlighten and liberate the workers of the world."

He went on for an hour. By the time he was done, all the cadets were sweating from standing at attention for so long. Two more commissars came in and separated them into companies. A senior lieutenant with a revolver at his waist and a rifle-bearing corporal at his side led each group to its barracks in a part of the camp separate from the enlisted men's quarters. Maurice followed his group to the second floor and put his few remaining belongings on one of the cots lined up in a row. The others set their things on the trunks at the end of their cots, or pressed photographs of mothers and girlfriends between the slats of the walls.

A shock froze Maurice when he looked at a cadet standing by the window. Drawn as if by electric charge, he stepped up to the young man, who turned toward him and gasped.

"Good lord," Maurice said in Ukrainian.

"You—you look exactly like me," the other man said.

The two men stared at each other, then stood back to look each other up and down. Other cadets noticed and started to laugh. "Hey, look at the twins," one of them said.

"Who are you?" Maurice asked, almost afraid to hear the answer.

"Hrech Kowalchuk," the other said. Maurice was relieved to hear the man's voice at least was distinct from his own. "From Kharkiv. Not too far from here. Who are you?"

"Maurice Bury. Ternopyl." He looked for a long time at Kowalchuk's face, still barely able to believe his eyes. From the look on Kowalchuk's face, he felt the same.

Both men felt almost as if they were looking into mirrors. They were so alike in their faces, build, the colour of their hair and eyes, even the shape of each feature on their face.

Their mutual fascination was broken when a corporal stepped into the barracks and bellowed. "*Attention.*" Most of the boys snapped to what they thought was attention as the lieutenant entered behind the corporal. He walked the length of the barracks, snarling at cadets who weren't standing straight enough or whose uniforms were out of place. Finished and dissatisfied with the company, he nodded at the corporal, who began calling the roll. When he was finished, the lieutenant ordered them to the parade ground, where a sergeant waited in a fatigue uniform. The sergeant led the cadets on a run. They jogged out the camp gates and down a muddy road for two kilometres (Maurice counted their steps) before he turned them around and jogged back to the camp.

The boys were exhausted, soaked and muddy. Maurice's uniform was splattered and his feet were sore from running in stiff new boots. They sergeant kept them going, and by the time they ran back through the camp gates, they were all sore.

Then came lunch. Salty soup, a plate of potatoes, bread and tea. After lunch, the officer cadets assembled in a classroom of long tables and chairs. Each got a notebook and a pencil and sat down to listen to a lecture about how to lead soldiers. When that was over, they trooped to another building, where instructors showed them how to take apart a rifle, clean it and assemble it again. Most of the cadets had grown up on farms and already knew about rifles and guns. Maurice paid close attention. The Russian rifle was cruder and simpler than the German make his mother owned.

Supper was boiled meat, potatoes and bread, followed by tea. After that, the lieutenant inspected their beds. He did not look pleased with Maurice's. "Uneven," he said. "Creased. What's this—mud on your boots? Cadet, you have no excuse for not cleaning your boots. You'll have an extra work detail tomorrow for that."

Maurice resolved never to let the lieutenant see mud on his boots or creases in his bedclothes again.

Before they could go to bed, the cadets had to hear another lecture on the benefits and glories of communism from yet another commissar, who told them how he had served in the Red Army during the Civil War. "I fought imperialists and capitalists, intent on recapturing their positions in order to renew their wealth and power on the backs of the working people. They had even set up a sham government in Ukraine, a puppet of the imperialist capitalists in England and America. But we defeated the Whites and united Little Russia and White Russia with Great Russia."

I don't buy it, Maurice thought. He could not think of one person happy to join Russia.

Finally, much too late, the cadets stumbled into their barracks and everyone collapsed, exhausted, onto their cots. Within minutes, snores filled the room.

Maurice had just closed his eyes as the opening door hit the wall hard enough to rattle it. The overhead light seared his eyes. He jumped out of bed. The un-curtained window was dark.

"Attention," a corporal bellowed as he stepped into the dorm and stood beside the door. The senior lieutenant came into the room with a captain Maurice hadn't seen before. He was tall and thin with cropped black hair. The peak of his officer's hat gleamed and the red star seemed to glow. His uniform was stiff and perfectly creased, and made him look simultaneously powerful and precise. *He looked as an officer should*, Maurice thought, embarrassed to be standing in his underwear.

"Inspection," the corporal yelled.

"The cadets are ready, Captain Slutsky," the lieutenant said. Maurice struggled to remember his name.

As the lieutenant had earlier, Captain Slutsky strode the length of the room, looking carefully at each man, his folded uniform, his boots, his kit. The captain did not say a word, but looked at the lieutenant, who jotted down notes on a clipboard.

When the captain came to Maurice, he looked disappointed. The lieutenant wrote something down.

Captain Slutsky left without saying a word. The lieutenant stood by the door, scribbling on his clipboard.

Two cadets sat on their cots.

"The cadet company has not been dismissed," the corporal shouted, and the two young men sprang to their feet again. The lieutenant pointed to them. "You and you, get dressed. You will stand guard duty tonight." The men groaned as they reached for their uniforms. "And tomorrow night." They did not groan again.

As the remaining cadets stood at stiff attention, the lieutenant told each one what to do to bring his belongings up to officer standards. Maurice knew what the lieutenant would say to him. He had just tossed his uniform over his trunk, without ensuring everything was folded just so. His boots were scuffed at the toes and still muddy.

He hurried to smooth his pants and wipe some of the mud off his boots while the lieutenant spoke with the other cadets. When the he looked at Maurice's uniform, Maurice knew he had failed to meet his standard.

"Fold it like you're going to wear it to your wedding tomorrow. You are training to be an officer. Your boots should shine." He moved on to the next cadet.

It took the cadets more than an hour to clean and fold their uniforms and tidy their cots to the lieutenant's satisfaction. They looked completely worn out, but the lieutenant seemed comfortable.

Finally, the lights went out and the cadets collapsed onto their cots again. Maurice wondered if the lieutenant planned midnight inspections every night.

Chapter 4: Red Army training camp

Akhtyrka, Ukraine 1941

A bugle blasted. Maurice opened one eye to orange sunlight and cold air streaming through the open window.

"God, I just closed my eyes for a second," someone said, groaning.

A sergeant stepped into the dormitory. "Get up. No time for lying around. Fall in outside."

Maurice pulled on his uniform and tried to smooth it out as he ran down the steps. The sun was just above the green fields as he fell into ranks with the other cadets. He expected the sergeant to lead the cadets to the mess hall for breakfast, but instead, he led them through jumping jacks, stretches and twists, and then a march out the camp gates and along dirt roads through endless muddy fields.

By the time they stumbled back into the camp, they were hot, dusty and parched. The sergeant shone with a layer of sweat, but otherwise showed no fatigue. "All you pussies have to toughen up for the Red Army. But since we feel sorry for you on your first day, we'll let you eat breakfast."

In the long wooden mess hall, they fell onto benches

and received a steaming bowl of kasha—porridge made from buckwheat—and tea.

Maurice's daily routine was now controlled by precise military rigour: after the marches and exercises at sunrise and porridge, lessons filled the morning. Commissars lectured on Communist dogma and the new structure of the army. Sergeants demonstrated handling weapons and older officers taught them military strategy and how to command men.

Lunch of soup, bread and tea led to more exercises all afternoon—hours of marching. Sometimes obstacle courses, where bullets zipped inches overhead as they crawled through mud and under barbed wire. Then more marching across fields and through forests until the cadets' heads and feet ached. Maurice had never felt so tired in his life.

Supper was more substantial, often a stew, lots of bread, lots of soup and tea from steaming samovars.

At night, the boys staggered back to their barracks, dirty, sweaty and exhausted. But they couldn't collapse into bed. They had to spend at least another hour cleaning up their uniforms and polishing their boots.

Worst for Maurice were his feet. They were hot and sore after the first kilometre of marching. When he pulled his socks off at the end of the day, sweat would drip from them onto the floor. He had to wring them out.

The lieutenant did another midnight inspection the second night, but after that, left the cadets to sleep through the next several nights. Most of the cadets had grown up on farms, so rising early was nothing new. They got used to the sadistic sergeants and officers who drilled them from noon until evening, practising charges and attacks with bayonets and rifles. But they hated the long marches. Hour after hour of marching in step with hundreds of other cadets, goose-stepping over and over, out across fields and along muddy roads and then back to the camp.

They marched in all weather. In March's freezing rain, shivering through muddy fields and icy forests. They marched through warming April until their legs ached and their feet blistered. They marched through farm fields and forests, waded through chest-deep freezing rivers. They marched until Maurice was sure he would fall down. But the officers never relented. "Get up," they screamed. "Run like men, not like little girls."

Even worse were the overnight marches. The sergeants would lead them in full kits, heavy packs on their backs, miles away from the training camp. Then, finding a spot suitably damp or rocky or otherwise uncomfortable, told them to make camp. Their tents were only large tarpaulins, stretched over enough damp ground to give shelter to twelve men, without even a ground sheet. Instead, each man used his *shenil*, or great-coat, which he carried rolled up like a blanket and slung over one shoulder. Under the tent, they dug a trench to hold their boots, packs and rifles, and six men slept on either side.

As the weather warmed, the overnight marches and camps became more bearable, until one night when Maurice and eleven others were settling down. Maurice had just stretched out on his shenil when someone complained.

"Good God, what's that smell?"

Maurice ignored him. Everyone was sweaty and dirty. Everyone smelled.

"Maurice, is that from your boots?" said the cadet next to the trench, a short Ukrainian from the north part of the country.

"Very funny, George."

"No, seriously. Maurice, your boots really stink."

Maurice looked up and his face reddened as he saw more and more of the cadets nod agreement or wrinkle their noses.

"Come on, boys, do they smell any worse than yours?"

"Yes, they do," George said. The others nodded. "I

won't be able to sleep with that smell in here."

Hrech picked up Maurice's boots and put them outside the tent. Maurice was embarrassed and angry, but it was true. His feet sweated more than anyone else's. No one else's socks dripped onto the floor at the end of the day. No one else could wring water out of them or poured puddles out of their boots.

No matter how often or how much he washed, scrubbed and rinsed his feet, they sweated so much during the long marches that his boots stank worse than any other cadet's. He left the boots outside the dormitory when they slept in camp, and outside the tent on marches.

After two weeks, the skin of his soles began to crack. It seemed minor at first—just a little rough skin. But the cracks spread and deepened until they made walking agony. Maurice went to the infirmary. The doctor was a kindly old man who did not listen very long. He glanced at Maurice's feet and handed him a small bottle of red liquid.

"Iodine," he said. "Put two drops into a basin of water and soak your feet for fifteen minutes every evening before bed. And change your socks frequently during the day."

Maurice next went to the quartermaster, a short man whose nose seemed to be trying to get into his mouth. He spoke with such a nasal whine, Maurice could barely understand him. "I need some extra socks," he said.

"You get just as many as any other cadet," the quartermaster said, trying to shoo Maurice out of the storeroom.

"You don't understand. Doctor's orders."

"I don't care." He tried to push the door closed, but Maurice pushed it open again.

"The captain said so." He lied.

"What captain?" the quartermaster asked, but there was fear in his beady eyes.

Maurice locked his eyes on the quartermaster's. "Captain Slutsky."

"Captain Slutsky said that?"

"Yes. He said to do whatever the doctor ordered." The quartermaster hesitated, but let the door open. Maurice stepped into the storeroom. "You know how the captain respects the doctor. Doctor knows best."

The quartermaster looked at Maurice for three long seconds, then smacked his fleshy lips twice, sniffed snot back into his throat and shuffled back along the shelves. He came back and put four pairs of white wool socks into Maurice's hands. "Okay. But don't tell any of the others about this."

"Thank you, comrade." Maurice had to repress a smile.

At first, the iodine solution stung Maurice's feet, but he endured the pain for the prescribed time. Over the next few weeks, the cracks began to clear up and the pain decreased. He never learned what the cause was, but his feet sweated less and, once they had a chance to air out, his boots didn't smell so bad. He kept changing his socks four times a day, and soon the boys stopped complaining when he didn't exile his boots overnight.

Chapter 5: Day pass

Ahktyrka, 1941

Maurice found he enjoyed the formal courses, when old captains and colonels lectured on the theory of war strategy, combat tactics, signals and codes. He thought the Soviet strategy, for all the Communist theory of breaking with old strictures, was so basic as to be almost primitive—it seemed to consist mostly of charging straight at the enemy.

"The attack begins with an artillery bombardment," a scarred colonel would say. According to theory, a Red Army attack centred on the idea of deep battle tactics, with extensive use of air power, artillery and tanks. But everyone knew the Red Army was short on cannons and tanks.

In the command of men, the Red Army was truly innovative—if not totally successful. Following Communist theory, the army dispensed with ranks in the 1930s. No officers, no distinctions between men and no discrimination between classes in the defence forces of the Union of Soviet Socialist Republic, the workers' and peasants' paradise. All soldiers were equal.

The absurdity of an army with no ranks and no officers did not deter the Communists from implementing the idea. They did have categories, however, and fourteen levels of commanders.

The Red Army had its first test in 1939, when it invaded and took the eastern half of Poland two weeks after the Germans seized the west. Then it invaded Finland in the Winter War from November 1939 to March 1940.

"In order to secure Leningrad, the Red Army's approach demonstrated the new deep battle tactics. We had three times as many men as the Finnish army, thirty times as many aircraft and a hundred times as many tanks," a commissar said. "The Winter War was a great victory for the workers' and peasants' state. The Red Army achieved all its objectives: land in Karelia, the northern shore of Lake Ladoga, the Hanko peninsula and islands in the Gulf of Finland."

His story left out Stalin's purge of thirty thousand generals and other officers in 1937, and the lopsided casualties of the Winter War. The Finns held off the Soviets for four months, dressing in white camouflage to carry out wicked guerrilla attacks on the invaders. By the end of the war, the Finns had lost twenty-five thousand men, thirty tanks and sixty-two aircraft. The Red Army lost five times as many men. Another two hundred thousand were wounded and more than five thousand captured.

More than three thousand five hundred tanks were destroyed and more than five hundred aircraft, a total of more than three hundred thousand casualties—a ratio of nearly five to one. The commissar also did not mention that the Red Army did not conquer all of Finland nor bring about a major political change in the country.

One consequence of the Winter War, though, was a reformation of the Red Army. It restored the ranks and discipline it had abolished after the Civil War. The ranks the Bolsheviks had once described as heritage of tsarism.

All the cadets learned to pretend to believe the commissars' description of history through the lens of communist theory. Hardest to swallow was the propaganda about the great friendship between the USSR and Germany following the Molotov-von Ribbentrop non-aggression pact. All the cadets knew war was coming. Maurice had read *Mein Kampf*, and knew Hitler's desire for Ukraine as a source of food, cheap labour and *lebensraum*—living space. The question was, what did Hitler plan to do with the Ukrainians?

A Russian cadet named Igor Systov liked to call the Ukrainian cadets *kokhol*, or farmer. It was a minor pejorative in Russian, and the Ukrainians would respond by calling the Russians *kotsap*, goat.

Systov was a short, wiry man with greasy black hair, a pointy nose and dark brown eyes. For some reason, Maurice was his favourite target for abuse.

"How are your shit-digging kokhol parents these days, Bury?" he asked every morning. "Don't worry," he would say, turning to his sniggering friends behind him. "He can't understand very well."

Most of the time, Maurice ignored Systov, even when he felt his head getting hot when Systov talked about his mother and sister. *How did he find out about my family?*

Maurice reached his breaking point in late March. The morning had begun with a brutal jog through deep, muddy slush and a late return to the camp. It meant cold porridge and tepid tea. In the afternoon, Maurice had trouble reassembling an anti-tank gun. His hands were clumsy with cold, and when he dropped a delicate part of the firing mechanism, the instructor screamed at him. "Don't be such an oaf. That gun will save your life one day."

Maurice put the gun together, brushed his hands off and asked permission to get a pair of gloves from his locker. Systov, standing with a group of other Russian cadets, watched him walking through the muddy grounds.

"Hey, kokhol, forget your shovel?"

Ignore the little turd, Maurice thought. But the turd persisted.

"Going to shovel the shit?"

"Shut up, comrade," Maurice said aloud. "I've had enough from you."

"Oh, the kokhol is testy today," Systov said to his friends. They laughed. Maurice thought then how bizarre it was that men who were training to kill and be killed were acting like school children. He continued toward the dormitory, taking long, slow breaths.

"Hey, kokhol Bury, you're heading the wrong way," the little turd said. "The manure pile is that way." He and his friends laughed again.

Maurice could feel his ears burning. He stepped toward the Russians. "For the last time, shut up," he said.

Cadets crowded around them, hoping for some diversion in the form of a scrap.

The little Russian stepped closer until he was looking up into Maurice's nostrils. "Tell me to shut up, kokhol? Don't you know your place? Don't talk to me like that, you hillbilly."

Maurice shoved Systov. The smaller man went down on his butt and sprang up again, swinging his fists at Maurice's stomach. His strength surprised Maurice and he nearly fell. He tried punching back, but Systov blocked his fists, dodged and jabbed hard at Maurice's face. Blood spurted out of his nose.

Maurice stepped back, spitting out blood. Then he stepped close, grabbed Systov's belt in one hand and his collar in the other. With strength that astonished him and the onlookers, he lifted Systov and dumped him head-first in a rain barrel. Systov's friends could not help but laugh as he kicked and shouted helplessly. They almost collapsed into hysteria when the barrel tipped over and rolled into a puddle. Systov kept kicking until two of his friends pulled him out.

Hrech Kowalchuk jogged up to Maurice and gave him a handkerchief to dab the blood from his mouth. He picked up a handful of clean, slushy snow to clean Maurice's uniform. "Hurry, the captain's coming."

Captain Slutsky strode around the building. "What happened here?" he asked. As always, his uniform was perfect, clean and pressed. The mud must have been afraid to stick to his boots.

"Comrade-Cadet Systov fell into the rain barrel," one of the Ukrainian cadets said.

Captain Slutsky knew a fight had broken out and was looking for someone who would admit it. Maurice was dabbing his nose, Hrech Kowalchuk was looking at him and the rest were trying hard not to look at anything.

Slutsky pointed at Maurice. "What happened to him?"

"Nosebleed, Comrade-Captain," Kowalchuk said. "My friend Comrade Kowalchuk is prone to nosebleeds."

Kowalchuk was counting on his and Bury's eerie resemblance to confuse the captain.

"I thought you were Kowalchuk," Slutsky said.

"No, sir, I am Cadet Maurice Bury," Kowalchuk said. "From Ternopyl."

The captain glared at both of them. "Clean yourself up," he said, then stomped away, muttering, "I can never tell you two apart."

Later in the barracks, Maurice asked Hrech why he lied to the captain.

Kowalchuk smiled. "In case he wants to punish you for fighting. He thinks it was I who was fighting Systov, and no one knows about any problem between him and me. So when the captain starts asking questions about the fight between Kowalchuk and Systov, the cadets will tell him there never was such as fight—and they'll be telling the truth. Soon, he'll be so fed up with the conflicting information, he'll give up."

"Or he'll figure out you lied to him, and punish you along with me and Systov."

Kowalchuk shrugged. "Maybe. But probably not. Even if he does, we'll end up peeling potatoes. Or standing a few extra turns of guard duty." He lay back on his cot as Maurice continued cleaning up. "You know, one day I think it will be important for us to be confused for one another."

Once a month, the cadets would get day passes to go to the town of Okhtyrka in small groups. The slip of paper clearly stated they had to return to the camp by 6 p.m., suppertime.

When it was Maurice's turn, he joined Hrech and two other young Ukrainian boys, Taras and Boris.

About forty kilometres from the Russian border, Okhtyrka was mostly a market town dominated by a seventeenth-century Cossack fortress and its inevitable cathedral. Maurice thought it looked poor in comparison to the relatively western Ukrainian cities like Ternopyl and Lvov, even compared to the village of Nastasciv.

They sat in a small restaurant and ordered kasha, sausage and what passed for coffee in the USSR. It wasn't very good, but after weeks of army food, it felt like a gourmet meal.

"Not like Mama makes," Taras said. He was a skinny boy who, like Maurice, came from western Ukraine.

They prowled the dirt streets, ogling girls and gazing into the windows of the few shops. The shelves were nearly bare. Taras bought a shawl. "For my Mama," he said. Boris and Hrech admired horses.

In the afternoon, they went to the canteen at the Communist Party building, ordering more sausages, bread and a jug of beer. Boris bought a drink for the bartender, and he and Taras sat at a table with some Russian soldiers. After two glasses of beer, they were singing in a combination of Russian and Ukrainian that became more confused with each following glass.

Later in the afternoon, when Maurice and his friends were working on their third jug of beer, a group of young women sat at a table. Maurice heard them speaking Ukrainian, rather than Russian. He made an effort to clear his head and walked over, pleased he didn't stumble or

waver.

"Good afternoon, lovelies," he said. He smiled at the prettiest woman, who wore a red kerchief over her deep brown hair. "Would you join us for something to drink?" He held out his hand to indicate his three friends.

"And who might you be? Soldiers?" the pretty woman asked, glancing at her companions.

"Not just soldiers," Maurice said, sitting in an empty chair. "We are officers in training at the Akhtyrka camp." He waved to his friends. Hrech came over and sat beside Maurice. Boris and Taras were too busy singing with the Russian soldiers.

"Are you twins?" one of the women asked.

Maurice and Hrech laughed. "No, not even related," Maurice said.

"I'm Ihor," Hrech said. Maurice couldn't help shooting him a puzzled look. *Why was Kowalchuk giving them a fake name?* "This is my less handsome lookalike, Nikolai. You can call him Niko." He held out his hand. "And what are your names?"

The pretty girl in the red kerchief took Hrech's hand delicately. "Kateryna," she said, then pointed to each of her friends in turn. "Elizabetta, Olha and Maria. We work at the cigarette factory. We usually stop here for a glass of tea on Fridays."

"Well, aren't we lucky to have come by on a Friday," Hrech said.

"But today is Thursday," Maurice said. The girls laughed, and Maurice and Hrech joined them.

"You'd like something stronger than tea, I'll bet," Maurice said. The girls laughed again, so Maurice went to the bar for a bottle of vodka and six small glasses. He looked over at Boris and Taras, who were drinking yet more beer. The singing got louder as he sat with Hrech and the girls.

The girls downed as many shots of vodka as Hrech and Maurice. They ordered bread and meat for all of them.

After they finished eating, Kateryna pulled off her kerchief. Later, she was sitting on Maurice's lap and Hrech had his arms around the shoulders of both Maria and Olha. The Russian soldiers who Boris and Taras had drunk with left, staggering out of the canteen. Taras came over to talk with drunken earnestness with Elizabetta, a short blond, like him. Boris slept face-down on the table the Russians has abandoned.

Kateryna laughed at some joke Maurice made. He leaned closer and rubbed his nose gently on her throat and passed his fingers through her long brown hair. Her kerchief sat crumpled on the table in front of her.

Maurice leaned a little closer and gently kissed Kateryna's throat. "Why Niko, you're fresh," she said, laughing. But she didn't pull away.

The next voice he heard was Hrech's husky whisper. "Niko, the time."

Maurice opened his eyes. The windows were completely dark. "Shit." He looked at the clock over the bar. It was past six. "Shit," he said again. "We're really late."

Hrech touched Kateryna on the shoulder. "I'm sorry, but we have to go back to the base." The girls were disappointed, but shrugged and put on their kerchiefs and coats and left. Hrech shook Boris awake and the four cadets stumbled to the door.

The bartender stepped in front of them. "You owe another two rubles."

"Huh? I thought we paid already…" Maurice said.

"Two rubles." The bartender would not move out of their way. Maurice felt certain they had paid in full. "For the bread and meat you ordered the girls," the bartender said. "And the vodka."

In 1941, two rubles were enough to buy two meals. Maurice dug into his pocket and found a few coins. "Come on, boys, let's pay up," he said. The four of them scrounged and finally gathered enough.

They stepped out onto the dirt street and pulled their thin jackets closer around themselves, shivering in the early springtime chill. Maurice had a feeling that being overcharged by the innkeeper was going to be their smallest problem that evening.

Chapter 6: In the hole

Akhtyrka, Ukraine, 1941

They shivered on their walk along the muddy roads. The early April night had brought a chill wind, and they were sober and hungry by the time they reached the camp gates. They knew the supper hour was long past, but Boris led them to the cadets' mess, anyway. "We're entitled to dinner," he said.

The mess hall was empty except for the chef and two assistant cooks who were cleaning the kitchen. "Hey, comrades, can we get a little to eat?" Maurice asked. The assistant looked up, surprised, then turned to the head chef, mouth gaping.

"It's too late, boys. Supper's over," the chef said, growling.

"Aww, come on, cookie, it's not that late. Supper's barely over. Come on, we're hungry."

But the chef just shook his head. "You know the rules as well as I do. You had time to come and eat. Now we're clearing up. Come back tomorrow, on time."

The cadets continued to protest. Maurice thought they could wear him down by complaining about how hungry they were, how little they'd eaten all day (which wasn't true) and how hard they would have to work tomorrow. But the chef only shook his head. Around him, his assistants continued to clean.

Taras started to get louder, and the chef got louder in return. Soon they were screaming at each other. "Get out of here," the chef bellowed finally, threatening the cadets with a raised ladle.

The door opened and Colonel Zayats, the camp commandant, stepped in. He was a young man with a serious manner. After Stalin's purges, Maurice knew, all the senior officers were young. His face was calm and in his long coat and perfectly pressed uniform, he looked elegant and controlled. "What is all this noise for?" he asked.

"We're just looking for supper, Comrade Commander," Maurice said, his heart slamming against his ribs.

The chef lowered his ladle. "These four are too late," he said. "Supper hour is over."

The commandant looked over the four cadets. "Give them something to eat, as much as they like," he said. "Then bring them to my quarters." He left.

The chef glared at the four cadets, then shouted at his assistants to bring four meals. The chef banged utensils and pots while an assistant brought our four bowls of soup, a loaf of bread and four plates of stew.

The four cadets ate quietly while the cooks finished cleaning up. The soup was lukewarm and the bread was stale, as usual. When they were done eating, they each took a cup of tepid tea from the samovar.

"If you're done eating, you can clean your own dishes," the chef said. He watched as the four cleaned up after themselves. He wiped the countertop one last time with his damp towel and scowled at the table they had vacated. Then he pulled on a coat and led the four to the commandant's quarters, a small, tidy house at the back of the camp.

They found the commandant sitting at a plain, army-issue desk, still in full dress uniform. In a hard chair beside the desk sat the head commissar, Linsky, a thin man with rimless glasses and an overbite.

"You were late," Linsky said after the chef left. The boys nodded. "You were given passes by Sergeant Jablonski to go to town, and you were told to return before 6 p.m.—before supper." The boys nodded again, but the commissar wasn't asking them.

"You have broken regulations, and you have also broken the trust placed in an officer. Your role is to set an example for the men, to uphold not only the regulations but also the moral standard essential for the morale of the fighting men and the victory of the Communist state."

"You will sit in solitary confinement for twenty-four hours," Colonel Zayats said. He nodded and two guards stepped forward, rifles ready. One led the cadets out of the commandant's quarters, and the other followed, to a small field behind the enlisted men's barracks.

One guard pointed at four small holes dug into the ground. The cadets understood immediately and each lowered himself into one. It was barely big enough to squat in, knees pressed into the dirt.

"Get your head down," a guard shouted. Maurice ducked just in time. The guard dropped a plank over the hole.

He could not stand up straight because the hole was not deep enough, nor could he sit, because the hole was not wide enough. Soon the moisture in the soil soaked through his uniform and he started to shiver. The air in the hole became stuffy. He tried to angle his head to bring his nose as close as possible to the narrow space between the top of the hole and the uneven plank, but all he succeeded in doing was hurting his neck.

"Hey, Maurice, you okay?" Taras said from the next hole.

"Shut up," the guard said, and stamped on the boards over Taras and Maurice, hurting their skulls. The four spent the rest of the night and the next day cramped, shivering, sweating, thirsty and hungry, until the cold evening came again. Finally, they heard Commissar Linsky's voice. "All right, you truants. Holiday's over. Get out of there."

The guards removed the boards, but Maurice could not stand up. Every muscle hurt. "Come on, you cunts, get out of there," Linsky yelled. The guards pointed their rifles at the cadets. With every motion and effort a distinct agony, the four managed to climb out and stand at something like attention.

"It's been less than twenty-four hours. We have taken a little time off your punishment so you don't inconvenience the chef again," Linsky said in his sombre, eerie way. His protruding teeth shone in the lamplight like the reflections in his glasses. "This is the last leniency you will see. Do not break regulations again."

The cadets staggered to the mess hall. The chef gloated and the other cadets smirked, but they had saved them each an extra cup of tea.

On the first warm morning of May, the cadets were surprised to find a new training leader in the parade ground. The boys were doubtful and suspicious of Lieutenant Ivan Petreshen. They dreaded the new tortures this slender blond Russian with the sensitive face would dream up, especially now that the weather held the promise of real summer heat. They expected more hours of drilling, marching and jogging and new kinds of exercises designed in headquarters to break young men's spirits.

"Good morning, comrades," Lieutenant Petreshen shouted cheerfully, hands on his hips. He was dressed in shorts and running shoes, and wore a light peaked cap on his head. "Are you ready for a long run?"

Kowalchuk groaned. "Shorts," he muttered so only Maurice could hear. "What's with this faggot?"

"Quiet in the ranks," the sergeant said. The cadets stood up straighter.

Lieutenant Petreshen laughed. "Come on now, we're going to have some fun." He started with jumping jacks, and the cadets had to suppress their groans as they followed him. Without slowing his pace, he said, "Two hundred of these." They were all out of breath by the time the sergeant finished counting.

Then without any warning, the lieutenant turned and ran for the gate. "Come *on*."

The sergeant bullied the cadets into a double line. Maurice began to doubt the new officer's sanity as they jogged behind the lieutenant. They went down the same paths they had worn over the past weeks, through the straggly forest of thin trees in new leaf. Then they left the familiar paths and stumbled down a slope to the banks of a stream.

Petreshen kept up a steady pace, but not a gruelling one. When they arrived in a clearing, Maurice expected they'd do drills, perhaps practise charging at each other or self-defence. Petersen's next instruction shocked all the cadets.

"Sit down, boys." The cadets looked at the lieutenant, then at each other. "Sit down," he said again. "We'll take a rest here. It's a hot day."

The cadets could not believe it. None of them had dared dream of the luxury of sitting on soft grass beside a stream on a hot May morning. One by one, they sat or fell back and took long, deep breaths. Maurice stretched his legs and turned his face to the sun. Soon they were laughing and talking easily, almost forgetting they were cadets of the Red Army. Some removed their boots and cooled their sore feet in the stream. Most just sat or lay in the grass and rested. A few even fell asleep.

The lieutenant let them rest all morning, until it was time to go back for lunch and their courses. Every day from that point, Lieutenant Petreshen led the company jogging out of the camp, at the same time the other companies jogged out. Each company went its own way. Sometimes along the roads, sometimes across fields, along streams, wherever the commander thought the boys needed training. Petreshen led his company in a different direction each day, but always out of sight of the camp and the other companies. Every day, he found a secluded spot to rest. "What's the point of marching and marching until we're all exhausted?" he said.

At the end of the exercise period, all the cadets would stagger back to the camp after hours of marching, drilling and jogging, and then would fall down with weariness. But Petreshen's boys always came back stepping high and singing. The officers and the other cadets were amazed at the group's stamina. They knew enough to stay silent about the lieutenant's kindness.

Chapter 7: Barbarossa

Eastern Ukraine, June 1941

The rests by the riverbank became shorter as the boys became conditioned. To boost their morale, the lieutenant led the cadets in singing old songs they all knew, even songs the commissars disapproved.

It worked. Maurice felt physically better than he ever had. His feet did not hurt anymore. Like the other cadets in his company, he stepped high, sang higher, looking up into the clear blue sky as they marched back to camp.

It was June 22. Maurice's company sang in harmony on the way back to camp. But the singing died as they passed through the gates. Junior officers and sergeants scurried back and forth and all the cadets gathered in front of the mess hall. The colonel stood in front of them, looking worried. But it was Linsky, the head commissar, who spoke. He read from telegrams in his hands, and the rest of the camp strained to hear him. "...all units in training will muster to operational status immediately. Form into operational groups without delay."

"What's going on?" someone asked.

Linsky looked up, annoyed. "For those who have just arrived, I have received urgent telegrams from central Party offices in Moscow." He paused, puffing out his chest. "The fascist German state has attacked across all our western frontiers, as of three o'clock this morning. Nazi Germany has declared war on the workers' and peasants' state.

"At several points along the frontier, German soldiers called to the Soviet border guards asking them to come out to hear some important news, then shot them without warning. The enemy has crossed the frontier and is now pressing eastward.

"Comrade Stalin has withdrawn to prepare plans for the annihilation of the invaders and the destruction of the bloodthirsty, fascist Hitlerite regime, and the liberation of workers from Poland to Berlin. All armed forces are ordered to mobilize."

Maurice realized he had stopped breathing. *This is it,* he thought. *Mother was right. I'm going to war.*

One week later, Maurice squinted through a narrow window-slit in an armoured rail car, trying to get a clear view of their situation. "Kyiv. The enemy's in Kyiv," someone said behind him.

"How the fuck do you know it's Kyiv?" someone else said.

"I grew up in Danyts'kyi. I know what Kyiv looks like."

"The city is on fire," a third man said. "The Germans have reached Kyiv already."

All Maurice could see were houses and fields. The train crawled forward like a dying, groaning beast. He pressed his face against the shaking wall of the car, but could not see much other than the buildings along the track.

The view opened up briefly as they entered a rail yard then pulled up beside another train. Maurice saw men climbing out of wagons and unloading weapons, equipment, carts, supplies and horses. Officers and commissars strode and shouted. From overhead, he heard planes droning and roaring.

He turned away from the scene outside as the train slowed more. As its noise subsided, he heard more from outside: banging and clanging, orders yelled and acknowledged.

In front of Maurice were eleven men, his command. He had met them two days ago at the Okhtyrka train station, and he struggled to remember all their names. They were all Ukrainian, as was the rest of the company—except for the commissars. Maurice scanned over them. Vasylko looked bored, Yosyp nervous, Alexey terrified. Between them were their crates of supplies, two-wheeled carts, ammunition and two dismantled anti-tank guns.

The train groaned, shuddered and threw everyone aboard forward then back, then forward again as it stopped. "Get off me, asshole," someone said. Someone else apologized. The door slid open to admit blinding sunshine and the tumult of an army assembling. Commissars ran along the train, banging on the wooden cars and yelling. "Out. Get off the train and assemble ready for action."

Two men shoved a ramp out the wagon doors. It was really just boards hammered together, sitting on the edge of the wagon, not attached to anything. The men picked up sacks and boxes and ran out, or in teams pulled out carts and heavy crates.

"Come on, boys, off the train," Maurice said.

My first order, he thought.

"Vasylko, Yosyp, Alexey, Myron, take the guns." His men scrambled, picked up their things and joined the chaos of men and equipment pushing down the ramp.

Maurice saw two of his men reach the ground and look around, unsure of what to do among the throngs pushing in every direction. "Keep our equipment together, get it set up for transport," he shouted to two men on the ground. *Basil and Lev?*

In the torrent of voices of men and horses and machine noise, a new drone pulled Maurice's eyes up. Beyond the rail yard, empty fields fell down toward the Dnipro River, and beyond that, the city of Kyiv. Above, in the blue sky, two airplanes flew straight toward them.

"Messerschmidts," someone yelled as the planes' drone became a scream. The chaos of an army disembarking from trains became panic.

The planes were almost on top of them in seconds. Dust and dirt puffed up from the ground in twin rows, ripping toward the trains. Maurice did not have time to think. "They're strafing us." Men fell, screaming.

Maurice jumped to the right in the same instant he saw the wooden side of the wagon burst. He felt a scorching pain across his left leg, just below the knee. He hit the ground, rolled and found he could not stand up.

Two of his men ran to him. "Lieutenant, you're hit," one shouted over the din. Anti-aircraft guns boomed. Little black clouds cracked uselessly after the Messerschmidts. Somewhere, an equally useless machine-gun rattled. The Messers banked, graceful as eagles as they turned away to the west.

Railcars burned. Beside the track, Maurice could see a sergeant striking soldiers, screaming at them for setting up a gun too slowly. "Fucking cowards."

The pain in his leg claimed his eyes again. His pant leg was ripped from his thigh to his ankle and his beautiful officer's boot was shredded. Blood poured down his shin, soaking the cloth and leather. He gently pushed the cloth away to see jagged chunks of wood and metal splinters embedded in his calf.

Seeing the wound intensified the pain. Maurice clenched his teeth. *If I start screaming,* he thought, *I'll never stop.* Two of his men picked him up under his arms and dragged him to a spot away from the burning train and the press of people.

"Get the others over here, and all the equipment," Maurice said. Soon, the company medic was pulling the larger pieces of shrapnel out of his leg, but he could not extract the small pieces deep in his flesh. The medic wound a cloth around Maurice's thigh. "You'll need to go to the hospital for that," he said. Then he swabbed at smaller wounds on each side of Maurice's jaw, where more shrapnel had scraped channels less than a centimetre from his jugular.

The captain appeared at his side. "Heard you've been hit," he said. He crouched to frown closer at the bandages, then straightened and held out his hands. "Medic says you'll have to go to the hospital. I think he's right." Maurice took the captain's hands and tried to stand. Pain lanced from ankle to his hip and into his back. His vision swam and blurred and he fell to the ground. He could feel blood flowing down his leg. "Don't try to get up, Bury," the captain said. "Stretcher!"

Two more men appeared beside Maurice. One took his ankles, the other his shoulders, and pain shot through his whole body again as they lifted and shifted him to one side. Maurice felt something give way in his leg. Blood spurted, and then his vision blurred again and went black.

He woke as men loaded him into the back of a truck, then blacked out again. Sounds and sensations came and went. He thought he felt hands on his leg, then tugging on his pants. Then something was on his face and something else pinched his arm, and everything was quiet and dark for a long time.

Moans and cries woke him. He opened his eyes to sunlight shining on a clean, white sheet. He hesitated to look at his leg, but it seemed to be whole. He pulled the sheet aside. His left leg was wrapped in white bandages from thigh to ankle, and suspended by straps to a harness over the foot of the bed.

Across a narrow aisle in front of his bed was another bed with another wounded man. Behind him, a streaked window let in yellow-gold sunlight, slanting through the ward in the early evening. Maurice could see thin, wispy clouds turned to pink and gold by the setting sun, and lower, darker clouds of smoke.

He turned toward the next bed, and saw a nurse—or

rather, her back. A thin, young girl in the blue-and-white uniform with red markings of the Communist party. "Where am I?" he said, croaking, shocked at the sound of his own voice. "How badly am I hurt?"

The nurse turned. She was a middle-aged woman, her dark hair streaked with grey. She smiled a little. "You're not so bad, son. You were lucky." She looked at his bandages. "The surgeon removed all the shrapnel. You'll be on your feet in another day or two." She turned away to tend to the next man.

Maurice tried to raise his head, but it was difficult because his leg was elevated. He could see the man in the next bed had no legs. The sheets lay flat on the mattress from the middle of his thighs. Maurice looked a little farther and saw every bed in the ward held a man covered in red-stained bandages. More men lay in stretchers between beds, against the walls and beyond the door in the hallway. He realized then the din of moaning and crying was loud. Men and women in uniform bustled around, carrying trays and instruments, bandages and bottles. It seemed from their terse conversations that they were short of everything.

With a shock, Maurice remembered his birth certificate. He tried to sit up, but the pain from his leg threw him back down. He looked left and right and saw the remains of his uniform folded on a little table to right of his bed.

Gritting his teeth against the pain in his leg, he twisted, reaching across his body for his shirt. Inside the pocket, he could feel a slip of paper. He peeked under the fold, saw part of the words "Dominion of Canada," and let his breath out again.

"Hey, you," a voice said to his right. Maurice let go of his shirt and looked up. The man in the next bed sat up, leaning on his elbows. Bandages swathed his head and one side of his face, covering one eye. "Got any cigarettes?"

"I don't know. I don't think so," Maurice said. "Anyway, I don't think we're allowed to smoke in a hospital."

The other man swept his hand in disgust. "What's your name?"

"Maurice Bury. Lieutenant. From Ternopyl."

"Pavel Shensky. Lieutenant, also. I'm from the Trans-Baikal. We just arrived here and got thrown into the fighting as soon as we got off the train. What a mess." He sighed.

"Me, too. My company just got here from Akhtyrka. I was hit by shrapnel even before I got off the train."

"So bloody disorganized. We got to Kyiv at the end of June. No sooner did we get off the train than we got back on again for Orel. We got as far as Shepetkova when we were bombed. We've been running and fighting all the way back here. We should have just stayed where we were."

Maurice did not know what to say. "We'll hold Kyiv," he said.

Shensky shook his head. "You haven't had a chance to really see the Germans in action, friend. They're unstoppable. They're a juggernaut."

"No one's invincible."

Shensky sat up again and glared at Maurice. "They took Poland in two weeks, France in less than that, and sent the English packing at the same time. How long did it take the Panzers to get from the border to Kyiv—three weeks? The only reason my army kept getting shuttled back and forth is because the bosses in Moscow can't decide which calamity needs reinforcement more—Moscow, Leningrad or Kyiv." He shook his head. "Face it, Bury. They haven't been beaten because they're unbeatable."

Maurice did not know what to say. He knew he couldn't admit his own ambivalence about the defeat of the communist Soviet Union and his disgust with Nazis. He couldn't talk to a Russian from the farthest reaches of Siberia, Trans-Baikal, about the national aspirations of Ukraine. He might even be a Communist Party member. And in the hospital, a commissar had to be nearby.

"So, you've seen them, the Germans?"

"We dug in north of Kyiv to stop them from getting to the bridgeheads. The Panzers raced right over us. Our guns were useless. Shells just bounced off the armour.

"My unit, twelve boys and me, we hid in a farmhouse and tried to pick off the infantry, but they're just about impossible to hit in their armoured cars. Then a tank shot right at the farmhouse. Damned shell went off in the second storey and brought down the whole roof on me. I lost an eye." He gestured weakly at his bandaged face. "And two fingers. Still, I was lucky. The rest of my unit was killed."

"I'm sorry," Maurice said. "I think my boys are okay—they were when they brought me to the medic. We were attacked by planes as we got off the train. I took shrapnel in my leg. Hurt like hell, but it's getting better. So I'm lucky, too."

"You're not as lucky as I am, friend," Shensky said, lying back and staring at the ceiling. "I'm finished. I'm going home. You'll recover completely. You're going back to the fighting."

Maurice did not answer. He felt exhausted. Shensky, too, had had enough of talking.

Sometime later, a doctor came by, checked his bandages, nodded at the nurse and turned to Shensky. Maurice heard a bustle at the ward doorway and a voice called out. "More wounded." Nurses and doctors scrambled out, leaving the previous batch of wounded to moan.

Maurice stared up at the ceiling, dozing off and on. Night fell and he slept until another nurse woke him with a wet cloth and a battered, stained tin bed pan.

Breakfast was kasha. Bland, sticky, almost inedible. Not like his mother's. Two nurses came after and changed his bandages, but that was almost the only human interaction Maurice had all morning. Shensky was not in a mood for talking. He stared with his one eye at his bedframe or the floor. The men in beds on either side of Maurice remained unconscious.

Looking out the window required Maurice to raise his head off the pillow a little, which was tiring after a time, so he stared at the ceiling, drifting off to sleep every so often. Eventually, lunch came—cabbage soup and black bread, a glass of water, biscuits for dessert. With his leg elevated, sitting up was even harder than lifting his head to look out the window. He had to hunch over the tray, and he flinched when the hot soup spilled onto his chest.

But the bread was fresh, and the biscuits surprisingly delicious. He would always remember them. "Better than the army, eh, Bury?" Shensky chuckled, coming out of his funk during the meal. "I can't wait to taste my mama's cabbage soup again, though."

"My mother is behind enemy lines," Maurice said.

Shensky did not say anything more all day.

Maurice watched the bright patch on the wall where the summer sun splashed through the window as it moved toward the hall door. Only orderlies handing out bedpans broke the monotony. Embarrassed, Maurice tried to raise the sheets for a little privacy, but relieving himself was painful and awkward with his leg elevated.

Supper was more soup, a small piece of meat and a small potato, bread, tea and more of those wonderful biscuits. After, his leg began to ache more intensely. He hesitated to call for a nurse when so many in the ward had worse wounds. The man beside him with no legs, Shensky had only one eye, a man beside him with one arm. Men bandaged and bleeding, crying and groaning. Orderlies pulled sheets over the heads of patients and carried their bodies out on stretchers, then replaced them with more wounded.

As the sky beyond the window darkened, nurses brought pills. "Aspirin," said a young girl, almost pretty. She tried to smile reassuringly, but Maurice could see she was close to tears. "Thanks. I feel better already," he said, but she didn't seem to hear him.

The aspirin was just starting to take the edge off the pain in Maurice's leg when a group of nurses entered the ward. They were older than the girl who had brought Maurice's pills and, from the looks on their faces, tougher. But they were also wearied by the unending stream of wounded. Bed by bed, the nurses worked their way from one end of the ward to the other, changing bandages, cleaning, doling out more pills, swabbing disinfectant. They occasionally exchanged a word or two to ask for gauze or disinfectant, once or twice to comfort a man.

Once, Maurice saw them shake their heads and pull a sheet over a soldier's face. In the next bed, two nurses held a screaming soldier's arms down so a third could clean his wounds. When the third nurse had rewrapped the stump of the man's leg, his screams turned into sobs. He fell back, defeated, and the nurses moved to the next bed.

When they reached Maurice, they lowered his leg from traction, changed the bandages in less than a minute, said a few words of encouragement, satisfied with the progress of his wounds, and moved across the aisle to Shensky.

When the nurses left, the lights went out for fear of air raids. There was nothing to do but sleep. The aspirin wore off after a couple of hours and Maurice woke again to the softer groans and weeping of the Red Army around him. He felt pressure in his bladder and groped for the bedpan. Sliding it carefully under the sheets, he felt almost proud of himself for peeing so neatly and quietly—until he spilled half the contents onto the floor.

Maurice awoke to the morning bustle: cleaning bedpans, fresh bandages, breakfast—tea and porridge again.

This became his routine: aspirin, bedpan, bandages, breakfast. He chatted occasionally with Shensky. Once a day, a doctor checked everyone, looked at bandages, read charts, exchanged terse phrases with the nurses. Each day, he would pat Maurice on the shoulder. "You're doing well, you'll be up and walking soon, Lieutenant," he would say.

The doctor did not inspire much confidence in Maurice—he was too young, too nervous. He was continually stopping in mid-stride, turning as if he had forgotten something, checking things he had already checked twice. He smiled too much, spoke too fast and either too loudly or softly. But when he spoke, he sounded positive, a confidence born from his fresh knowledge of all his medical textbooks.

On Maurice's second afternoon in the hospital, the man to Maurice's right woke with a snort and started screaming. "My legs! Oh my God, my legs! My legs are gone!" A nurse rushed to his bed and held something over his face until he slumped, unconscious again. Evening fell before the man woke again.

"Don't scream," Maurice said. "It won't help. Yes, your legs are gone. I'm sorry."

The other man wept. "My legs. The airplanes, the bombs were so close…"

"At least you're alive," Maurice said. "I saw a lot of men die on the field and in here. You're still alive, and soon you'll go home."

"Without my legs? How can I work on a farm with no legs? Oh, god. Why didn't I die?"

"What's your name?" Maurice was desperate to stop the man's crying. But the man ignored him. Even though Maurice and Shensky tried through the day to engage him in conversation, he would only turn away to mourn the loss of his limbs. Two days later, soldiers took him away on a stretcher, telling him he would be boarding one of the few trains going east. During the rest of Maurice's stay, that bed would be filled with a succession of wounded men, each more gruesome than the last.

By the third day, the pain in Maurice's foot changed to numbness. After the nurse unwrapped the bandage, she looked at his left foot, which was swollen and dark, like a big bruise. Maurice knew enough about anatomy and medicine from his preliminary, truncated studies in Peremyshl to fear the blackening of his foot.

"Can you move your toes?" the nurse asked.

Maurice failed. "I cannot feel them."

The nurse felt his foot the way a mother touches her child's forehead to detect a fever. "Don't worry," she said, rewrapped the bandage around his knee. She left the ward quickly.

Maurice felt his heart pounding. *I can't let fear break me down,* he thought, *not after my speech to the man who had lost his legs.*

The nurse came back with the young doctor in tow. He bent low over Maurice's foot, poked the top, asked Maurice to wiggle his toes. This time, they twitched a little. "This foot is going to have to come off," he said.

"No, Doctor, please."

The doctor looked up. "It's going gangrenous. It will turn to necrosis and spread. Amputation is the only way to stop it."

"No, please. There must be something else you can do." Maurice tried to wiggle his toes again.

"I'll ask my colleague. But don't get your hopes up."

Maurice slumped back and stared at the ceiling. He tried to make his mind go blank, but could not. Losing his foot, he'd be a cripple. Would the doctors give him some kind of prosthesis?

An older doctor came the next day. His mouth turned down as he inspected Maurice's black foot. He shook his head.

"Please don't cut off my foot," Maurice said, but there was no hope in his voice.

The doctor shook his head again. "It should come off. The necrosis will spread, you know."

"But it's not dead," Maurice said. He wiggled his toes again a little. "Isn't there anything else you can try?"

The doctor sighed. "Well, we can try. But I don't think

it will work." He left, and Maurice alternated between faint hope and deep despair.

The doctor returned, an orderly behind him, lugging two heavy buckets of water, which he set beside Maurice's bed. "Put your foot into this one, first," the doctor said.

Maurice complied. The water was almost boiling hot.

"Push it down and hold it in as long as you can stand it."

Maurice could not stand it even for a solid minute.

"Now, put your foot into the other bucket."

The second bucket was icy cold, almost as painful as the hot.

"Now, keep your foot there for five minutes. Then back into the hot. Back and forth, up to five minutes at a time, or as long as you can stand it," the doctor said. "Keep doing that three times a day." He instructed the orderly to bring buckets three times a day, then disappeared. Maurice never saw him again.

For another week, the orderly followed the doctor's orders. Maurice found he could keep his foot in the hot water for longer and longer periods after the first immersion. He wondered whether this was an actual treatment or if the doctor was just humouring him. As if to say, "Look, soldier, your foot is dead. You don't even feel water."

But the foot responded. On the third day of treatment, Maurice thought its colour looked a little lighter. There seemed to be pinkish patches on top. The next day, he could move his toes a little, and the day after, a little more.

Even the nurses agreed with him. "Yes, it looks much better, Merosho," said the oldest one, using a pet name for him even his mother didn't use anymore.

A few days later, the young doctor came back as Maurice was soaking his foot in hot water. "How is it?" he asked, frowning at the buckets.

Maurice lifted his foot for the doctor. "Much better. Look." He wiggled his toes successfully.

The doctor crouched for a better look. He pushed the toes back and forth. Maurice gathered his nerve to take a critical look, himself. Wishful thinking? No, the pink tone was definitely back. There were large grey areas on the skin, but no more black.

The doctor grunted and straightened. "Good. Stop taking the medicine. There is not enough to go around."

The next day, despite the pain—mostly from disuse, the doctor said —Maurice stood and even took a few steps. That became another part of his daily routine. Three times a day, before each meal, Maurice took a few steps. A few more each time until he was walking the length of the ward. Soon, he limped out into the hallway, where he almost toppled over wounded men lying on the floor, waiting for beds or assessment.

Shensky went home after a week. His bed was taken by a man who never woke up.

A week after that, the doctor watched Maurice walk from one end of the ward to the next, barely limping. "Congratulations, Lieutenant. You've earned the right to go to the front again."

What the hell do you know about the front? Maurice thought. *For that matter, what do I know about it?*

The next morning, Maurice ate his kasha, washed up thoroughly and dressed in a new uniform. He made certain to take his Canadian birth certificate from his old shirt and tucked it into the pocket of the new one. He pulled on a pair of soldier's felt boots and stood as the young doctor gave him a hospital discharge on a slip of paper. He took Maurice to the ground floor and pointed to an officer near the front door. "Report there," he said.

An official gave him another form, acknowledging the hospital discharge. "Give that to the commander of the army base," he said, and directed him out the door, where a horse-drawn wagon waited with a group of discharged patients. *I guess that's what's taking me to the base.*

Beside the door, Maurice saw a rolling cart stacked with

meals for patients. He snatched two more biscuits and shoved them into his pocket, and stepped into sunshine to return to war.

Chapter 8: Fighting on the Dnipro

Central Ukraine, September 1941

The Red Army's camps were not elaborate. Only the senior officers had tents or formal quarters of any kind. The mass of soldiers slept on the ground in groups of three. They would pool their *shenils*, or greatcoats, laying one on the ground and making a tiny tent with the other two propped up by their rifles. It was not much of a shelter, especially in cold weather, but it was better than nothing.

The wagon had taken Maurice and his fellow discharged patients from the hospital a few miles east of Kyiv. All through the journey, they could hear distant guns and see puffs of black clouds. The Germans had been threatening the Ukrainian capital since late July. Only when it was too late would the Red Army realize the enemy had been pushing deep both north and south of the city. Soon, the two German penetrations would encircle the city before a vicious fight.

The camp appeared in good order, Maurice thought. Weapons were stacked neatly, with the larger guns and their ammunition arranged on wagons. Horses stood, eating in little stockades arranged all around the camp.

There was no fence, no barrier between the campground and the empty farmland it had taken over. Wheat stood high and yellow under the summer sun. But as Maurice and a small group of men discharged from the hospital crossed an invisible boundary, they found two armed guards in front of them.

"Welcome to the 38th Army," one said, a corporal. "You are now under the command of General Feklenko."

"What happened to the 26th?" a major beside Maurice asked.

"The 38th Army was taken from the 26th," the corporal said. "Come with me to the major and we'll get you sorted out."

The corporal led them to a large tent guarded by two soldiers with rifles. Inside, a major sat behind a table with a pile of papers. A sergeant stood beside the table and spoke for the major, directing each of the recovered men to a different company.

The sergeant asked Maurice for his name. "Bury, Lieutenant."

The major looked up. "Are you Ukrainian?" he asked. Maurice nodded. "There's a unit of anti-tank gunners, fresh draftees from Ternopyl, who need a third lieutenant. Sergeant, send Lieutenant Bury there."

The sergeant nodded at a corporal, who took Maurice through the maze of arms and equipment. They arrived at a group of men gathered around a teepee of rifles, a small campfire, two disassembled anti-tank guns and a stack of ammunition crates.

"Here's your new lieutenant," the corporal said to a young sergeant, a fit-looking man with brown hair and thin lips. He leaned against a bale of straw, smoking a cigarette.

The corporal walked away without another word. Maurice and the sergeant looked at each other for a minute, and then the sergeant stood up straight and saluted. He dropped his cigarette and tried to stamp it out.

All around, the other men stood up, too and saluted.

Maurice saluted back. "I'm Lieutenant Bury, tovarisch. Can you please introduce me to the men?"

There were eleven men, a unit called an *odalenye.* It consisted of one sergeant, Petro; three corporals, Orest, Adam and Andrei; and seven privates. Maurice concentrated to remember their names: Viktor, Michael, Jarolsav, Yuri, Vyacheslav, Slawko and Big Eugene. They were all commanded by a third lieutenant—Maurice. He tried to impress them by inspecting the guns and ammunition, the men's uniforms and kits.

The unit was outfitted with three PPRD-41 anti-tank rifles. This was an odd-looking weapon. It looked like a large hunting rifle with a long, almost delicate barrel and a pistol-like hand-grip and trigger. A V-shaped stand held the far end of the barrel off the ground. Its ammunition appeared too small to have any effect on a tank, but it was designed to penetrate steel plate before exploding.

Operating the PTRD-41 required two men. One private loaded the ammunition into the breach, and a corporal aimed and fired the gun at the lieutenant's command. Its length, weight and lack of telescopic sights made it difficult to aim. Maurice knew every shot produced a huge muzzle blast and kicked up enough dirt to give away its position to the enemy.

He saw his main goal as commander of this anti-tank unit to keep the men alive. *The damn weapons make that a lot harder*, he thought.

The inspection complete, Maurice wondered what to do next. He decided to set up his own quarters, so he asked Corporal Orest, a thin boy no more than nineteen years old, to take him to the quartermaster. After some arguing, he got a new pair of pants fit for an officer, proper leather officer's boots and a new kit, including a new sidearm.

Lunchtime meant the boys, in shifts, went to one of several meal wagons for soup, bread and thin, foul-tasting tea. Maurice went to the "officers' mess," the large tent where the major had greeted him. The food wasn't much better. But it was a chance to meet the two other junior lieutenants in his company, young men like him. Vasyl and Danylo were two more Ukrainian boys fighting on Ukrainian territory for Russia. Together, their three *odalenye* made up a *rota*, which was led by a senior lieutenant, Igor Lobuvitsky, a short but burly man who was already going grey at less than thirty years old.

After lunch, all the lieutenants met at the Captain Tulub's command tent for orders. This was Maurice's first encounter with the company commissar, a small, thin and intense man named Matvienko. He had the broad face, dark brown eyes and cropped brown hair of a typical Russian. Like all commissars, he was a dedicated, almost fanatical Communist. But he was smarter than the first lieutenant and the captain.

After the obligatory pronouncements about the righteousness of the struggle against the fascists, he shut up and let the captain give the orders. They were moving at night, eastward and south to the Dnipro River, toward Kremenchuk, to take positions against the enemy's advance for the bridgeheads.

"And we're moving at night only, comrades," the captain said. "Maximum camouflage during the day."

That night, the men loaded up, carrying the disassembled anti-tank guns among themselves. With few lights and making as little noise as they could, the army started marching southeast, along dirt roads and over fields.

Marching at night was not easy. Maurice had never heard as much racket as when the army tried to move silently. The men cursed as they tripped over uneven ground and bumped into unseen obstacles. The wagons and equipment crashed as they rolled along. Non-commissioned officers berated the soldiers for not being quiet. Maurice stumbled repeatedly in holes in the road, and more than once caught one of his men from falling under the weight of the gun or ammunition.

In 1941, few roads across the Ukrainian countryside were paved. Most highways were three lanes of packed earth, raised a half-metre or so above the flat fields and covered with a thin layer of oiled gravel. Traffic would use one lane until it was so pot-holed and scarred that it was virtually impassable, then switch to the second until it was wrecked, too, and then move to the third. In the meantime, road crews had the chance to repair the first and second lanes. In effect, most roads were in poor condition most of the time. In late summer, they were at least solid, baked hard by the heat and the sun. But they were pitted, scored and ridged by the continuing passage of hundreds of trucks, tanks and wagons, tens of thousands of horses and millions of men.

A week passed before a grey dawn saw the 38th Army approach the western edge of Kremenchuk. The local population had dug trenches into high ground that overlooked a gentle slope toward the broad expanse of the Dnipro. The army settled in to wait for the Germans.

The broad Dnipro River is the middle of Ukraine. The capital, Kyiv, straddles the river, while the city of Kremenchuk, 300 kilometres southeast and downriver, sits on the left or eastern bank.

Maurice looked west, across the river.

"That's where the enemy is," Captain Tulub said. He was a small man even younger than Maurice. He pointed to a black cloud only a few miles back. "The Red 6th Army is fighting in Bila Tserkva (White Church)."

That meant the Germans had already penetrated nearly a thousand kilometers from the frontier in less than three months.

How could an army conquer half the territory of Ukraine that fast?

Commissar Matvienko appeared behind Maurice's shoulder. "The brave Red Army is inflicting heavy losses on the Nazis," he said, gazing to the west.

It would turn out to be true, but Maurice only learned that years later.

The locals had built bunkers under the trenches. The whole company, all three odalenye, thirty-six men and three officers, shared one room for sleeping. They stored their food and ammunition in another compartment. Quartermasters and cooks moved along the trenches and underground corridors to distribute supplies and food.

Maurice supervised as his men set up their guns overlooking a road that led to a narrow wooden bridge over the Dnipro River. He wondered if it could support a tank or an army. He also wondered what preparations the army had made for destroying it should the Germans break through here.

The army established its routine immediately. Daily, Maurice roused his men, breakfasted with the officers on porridge and tea, inspected the weapons and spent the day gazing across the broad river. He thought of his mother and sister in occupied Halychyna, of his father presumably in Montreal, and how agonizing it was that they could not communicate with one another, let each other know they were alive. He forced himself to believe his family was safe.

After a few days, the younger corporal, Orest, pointed out a low cloud getting closer. "The Germans are coming," he said. Soon, official word confirmed it. General Von Kleist had outflanked the Soviet 6th Army and his Panzers approached the Dnipro River. By early August, the Panzers encircled the 6th and 12th Soviet Armies near Uman in central Ukraine, killing or taking prisoner more than two hundred thousand Red Army soldiers.

On the bank of the Dnipro, officers ordered the men to blend into the landscape as well as they could—a tactic the Germans came to fear throughout the war.

Waiting for attack, Maurice and his men grew more and more nervous as the clouds approached the riverbank. By afternoon, they saw refugees approaching the bridges, streams of people on horse-drawn carts or on foot, a few rickety trucks. Behind them were the remnants of the 6th Army, mostly foot soldiers, a few battered tanks and hundreds of horse-drawn carts. From their vantage point, Maurice and his boys watched the sorry parade stream across the Dnipro bridges.

Then they heard the distant thunder of approaching war. And the Germans were upon them.

The airplanes were first. Maurice could never forget the buzzing sound of the Messerschmidts and the screaming Stuka bombers. They filled the sky, bombing and strafing, easily dodging Soviet anti-aircraft fire from the eastern riverbank.

"Where are our planes?" someone yelled after a bomb shook the bunkers.

There wasn't a Soviet aircraft to be seen—just panic on the ground as the guards blocked the bridges.

The Wehrmacht tore apart the ragged Soviet columns still on the western bank. Then Maurice and his men saw the dreaded Panzers. Some raced along the roads. Others crossed the deserted farmlands more slowly. It seemed only minutes before they were at the edge of the river, even though Maurice knew it had to have been hours.

Charges under the bridges detonated before the Germans got there, stranding thousands of refugees.

"The idiots," said Danylo, the lieutenant of the unit to Maurice's right. "They should have waited until the first tanks were halfway across and taken some of them down."

But Maurice and everyone else knew that was too risky.

Behind them, the Soviet heavy artillery started firing. Maurice saw plumes of dust rising as the shells struck among the German tanks but never actually hit one.

Behind the tanks came the infantry in squat armoured cars, and horses hauling cannons and wagons. By nightfall, the Germans had dug in behind the riverbank, and even though the Soviets kept firing cannons and mortars at them, the Germans didn't seem bothered. "They're indestructible," Private Yuri said. "We can't even touch them."

"Don't be stupid," Big Eugene said. He was a broad-shouldered youth who stood more than six feet tall. "Our gunners just have to get the range."

"Well, they sure seem to be having trouble doing that," Yuri said.

The Red Army settled into a new routine, hunkered down in the trenches during most of the day as each side's artillery duelled. Sometimes, the riflemen would take long shots at their opponents, but never hit anything. Overhead, the cannons and mortars roared and coughed and below the bluff, the shells exploded among the trucks and tanks. Occasionally, they hit something, but usually did no more than send dirt high into the air.

The Germans' heavy guns would answer, spitting death overhead to crash down behind them. Usually they missed, but sometimes they smashed apart stores of food or ammunition, sometimes ripping apart men and horses. Once, Maurice and his men rushed up the bank to help douse a fire burning close to an ammunition store.

Days dragged. Maurice and his unit spent as much time away from the trench as the officers would tolerate. They hid in the bunker, playing cards and smoking. While on duty, watching the enemy across the river, they felt useless.

"Why don't we attack them?" Corporal Orest said. "We're doing nothing. We have the higher ground. We could destroy them."

"Let's keep our heads down, Corporal," Maurice said. "There's no use in making ourselves into target practice for Fritz."

Or being cannon fodder for the Russians, he thought.

Matvienko or another commissar would regularly inspect their unit's battle-readiness, making sure every piece of equipment was clean and in its proper place. Most important, they made sure no one was having cowardly, deserting or politically incorrect thoughts.

"We're as dedicated to the cause of the people as you are, tovarisch," Maurice would say.

Matvienko didn't look like he believed him, but he didn't argue. He had other worries. More than any other officer, he kept the company ready for fighting.

By the middle of August, the Germans seemed to have finished whatever business lay behind them and turned their full attention on crossing the Dnipro. Although Maurice didn't know it, von Kleist's Panzers had already crossed the great river north of Kyiv and were racing for east Ukraine. Now the enemy below Maurice's position was getting ready to be the southern arm in another of the Wehrmacht's "pincer movements"—where two groups would penetrate deep into the Soviet lines, then turn toward each other to encircle whole Soviet armies.

The Stuka dive-bombers struck at dawn, shaking Maurice and his boys out of restless sleep in the bunker. Scrambling to pull on helmets, the boys crawled out of the trench to see hell erupt around them.

The noise would remain as one of Maurice's most awful memories of the war: screaming airplanes, whistling bombs, crashing explosions. And in response, the anti-aircraft guns crackled and the mortars and cannons boomed.

German airplanes filled the sky, dive-bombers and fighters banking and diving between the black clouds of anti-aircraft flack. The Stukas screamed as they dove to deliver their bombs to pinpoint targets. The explosions behind them rocked the bluff. Some of the boys tried to retreat to the bunker, but Maurice ordered them out again in case the bunker collapsed. He wondered which place, trench or bunker, was riskier. He concluded that at least in the trench he could see what the enemy was doing.

It was hard to see much of anything in the smoke and dust. He barely dared raise his head enough to peek over the lip of the trench. But from what he could make out, the Germans below did not seem to be doing much, yet.

"Over there, Lieutenant," Orest said, pointing downriver. Through the smoke, they could see trucks, tanks and some other, strange vehicles at the edge of the water. Men milled around and Maurice realized they were laying a pontoon bridge. River water geysered up as Soviet mortars tried to drive them away, but even that did not deter the German engineers. The bridge slowly and steadily took shape, reaching like a monstrous tongue across the river.

And still the German airplanes flew out of the west, dropping death. Maurice wondered if they landed, picked up more bombs and fuel and returned again. They must have, for the air raid went on all day long. Not once did anyone see a Red Army plane. Only occasionally did the anti-aircraft fire find its target and bring one of the bombers or fighters down. And still the German planes came, wave after wave, until nightfall.

That was when the German artillery started firing. First flares burned high and cast a brilliant, sickening light as they fell in dozens or hundreds, illuminating the Soviet positions. Then an almost simultaneous roar from scores of guns, and the explosions tore into the bluff and the high ground behind it. Torrents of dirt fell on the Soviet men.

"Keep down, boys," Maurice shouted, but they knew that already.

The Soviet heavy guns behind them answered almost immediately, but raggedly, one at a time, not in the concert like the Germans.

The artillery duel over the river lasted two full days. The Germans lit the Soviet shore with flares all night long, firing almost continuously. The Soviets answered as best they could, until a huge explosion behind the bluff told the Red soldiers a heavy gun had been knocked out by an accurate German shot.

Throughout the bombardment, all the regiments kept down in the trenches, sipping what water they had and eating crusts of dried bread from their packs. There was no other food. The cooks couldn't set up a kitchen and no one could move. The farthest corner of the trench became the latrine, and soon the smell made everyone gag. No one dared lift their heads over the edge of the trench.

Finally, on the third morning, the cannon fire died down.

"Have they run out of shells?" someone said.

"Maybe," said Petro, the sergeant. "They could just be waiting for more supplies."

The Soviet guns quieted, too.

Maurice chanced a peek above the lip of the trench. Across the river, the smoke was gradually clearing. He could just make out furious activity behind the German lines.

"It looks like they're moving out, heading south," Petro said, peering beside him.

Maurice nodded. But what did it mean?

The answer came in just a few minutes from a runner down the trench.

"We're moving out, withdrawing," he said breathlessly. "Captain just got his orders. Pack up and get ready to move down-river."

Chapter 9: Scorched earth

Ukraine, July 1941

No one said "retreat" or "strategic withdrawal," but the whole 38th Army moved east. What they were really trying to do was get in front of the Germans, which meant abandoning their positions on the Dnipro River, the heart of Ukraine. This left huge expanses to the enemy and meant destroying anything the Germans might be able to use.

There were many reasons for the Soviets' collapse. They continued to reel from the shock of Nazi Germany's surprise attack on June 22. The Red Army was unprepared for modern war, and Stalin refused, over and over again, to allow strategic withdrawals that would have allowed the Red Army to shore up defences further back from the invaders. Stalin instead ordered every man to fight to the death, not to give in to the enemy. Hundreds of thousands of soldiers died, were trapped and taken prisoner or despairing, surrendered with guns and tanks and armour intact.

Maurice and Petro carefully supervised the boys' packing-up. They would have no transport now, not even horses. They would have to carry the anti-tank guns, ammunition and supplies themselves. They men grumbled, but only a little.

By mid-morning, they were marching southeast. Periodically, messengers ran up with orders passed down from the captains, majors and colonels from Moscow and Comrade Stalin. "The enemy must not be left a single engine, a single railway truck, not a single pound of grain or gallon of fuel. Collective farmers must drive off all their cattle and turn over their grain to the safekeeping of the state authorities for transportation to the rear. Valuable property that cannot be withdrawn must be destroyed without fail."

Stalin had broadcast those words, intending to rouse the people. He hoped to invoke the collective memory of the scorched-earth retreat that defeated Napoleon's invasion in the previous century.

Contrary to later myth, though, the Red Army did not burn every building in advance of the Germans. In retreat, the Soviet soldiers marched into villages, bashed in doors and ordered the farmers out, giving them moments to snatch a few belongings. The soldiers commandeered men and boys to load food, animal feed and fuel onto army wagons. Usually, the army took the farmers' wagons and horses too, but Captain Tulub always let the farmers take a couple of animals and at least a wagon to load their things and flee east, ahead of the army.

The Red Army torched the occasional house if a commissar thought it might be of use to the Germans. They set fields alight, burned stacked hay and straw. The soldiers also had the chore of driving the pigs, cattle, sheep and horses head of them. "No use feeding Fritz," a commissar said, in a futile attempt at humour. Soldiers carrying guns and ammunition tried their best to herd the animals ahead, which slowed their progress even more.

Somehow, Maurice kept his boys together in the noisy, smelly mass of moving, shifting soldiers, civilians and animals. It looked chaotic at first glance, but Maurice could see some order. The traumatized civilians faced the loss of their homes and livelihoods with courage and dignity.

Sergeant Petro proved invaluable during the marches, and during the days when they hid. He kept the unit supplied with food, water and ammunition, when some units went without. He managed to scrounge up new felt boots when Big Eugene's wore out, and they almost fit, too.

"How did you get this?" Maurice asked more than once.

Petro would smile a little and wink. "I have my ways."

While their orders were to move only at night, it was next to impossible with the refugees and animals. Children cried when they couldn't rest at night and the animals got lost. By the second morning of withdrawal, they started moving again in full daylight.

By noon, Maurice tried to hustle his boys ahead. "We don't want to be at the back of the line when the Panzers come," he said.

The boys grumbled, but moved their feet faster.

As they passed an abandoned farm, Maurice heard shouts. A half-dozen men in NKVD uniforms aimed their rifles at an unusually large haystack. A commissar kicked it savagely, pistol in hand, screaming obscenities. "You cowards. Traitors." He kicked again as a man became visible under the straw. "Get out of there, all of you."

"Don't stop," Maurice said to his men. They continued walking, watching the tableau but not daring to look directly at it. The NKVD men ignored them.

Four Red Army soldiers climbed out of the haystack without weapons or hats. They raised trembling hands over their heads, straw falling from them like water. *Are they even eighteen years old?* Maurice wondered.

One man dropped to his knees. Maurice could see the tears on his cheeks. The commissar fired his pistol directly into his head. Before Maurice's heart could beat one more time, the other NKVD men had shot the rest of the deserters. Four shots, *bang-bang-bang-bang,* four bodies falling. The agents slung their rifles over their shoulders. The commissar holstered his pistol. He looked at Maurice's unit, carrying its anti-tank guns and driving a few sheep and pigs ahead of them. Maurice walked faster, looking straight ahead. The NKVD men lost interest in them. The commissar pointed at the farmhouse and two men set fire to it.

Maurice kept marching.

They caught up with the rest of the rota just after lunch, after all the other units had eaten their meagre field rations of bread and tea. The captain barked at them to settle into yet another set of trenches prepared by the locals, while the civilians kept going east. Three boys set up the gun and their equipment in a trench, but there was no bunker this time. Bohdan led the rest farther to the rear to find a place for a rudimentary camp. As in the camp outside Kyiv, the men grouped into threes to use their coats as makeshift tents.

Maurice found the field kitchen, a wooden horse-cart with a charcoal stove. A thin, homey wisp of smoke came out of a battered tin chimney. The cook was starting to clear his things away as Maurice begged for meals for his unit.

"You're late," the cook said without looking up.

"Yes, we've been marching as fast as we can," he said, but then remembered he was an officer. "Rations for one odalenje, comrade corporal," he said in his best officer's voice.

"No. You're too late. Lunch is over."

"Rations for twelve, now, corporal." Maurice tried to be threatening. He rested his hand on his sidearm. "That's an order."

Commissar Matvienko wandered up with a quizzical look on his face. He said nothing, but the cook looked at him. The commissar nodded with a strange smile.

The cook grumbled and set out his utensils again. Maurice called Viktor over and told him to bring the boys in for lunch. They came with their tin bowls and cups ready and walked away with their poor lunch: bread, tea, a small bowl of soup.

The cook swore under his breath continually and glared at Maurice whenever Commissar Matvienko was not looking. When the commissar left for the officer's tent, the cook came up to Maurice. "Listen to me, tovarisch lieutenant," he said, growling. "I don't care if you are an officer. This is the fucking army, for God's sake, so get your boys to the food wagon on time. I have to get my helpers together to start making supper now, and it's going to be late because of you and your boys. Do you think..."

A sudden roaring buzz drowned out the rest. Maurice felt a tug on his arm as Sergeant Petro pulled him to a trench and threw him in, jumping after him. The food wagon exploded into a burning shower of splinters. Overhead, a grey airplane climbed higher, banking to head back west.

Maurice and Bohdan climbed out of the trench and looked for the cook. They found him, face down on the ground and helped him up. He was dirty and shaken, but unhurt. He looked at the burning wreckage of his wagon and shook his head.

"Fucking Fritz," he muttered.

Chapter 10: Panzers

North of Poltava, Ukraine, October, 1941

Kyiv was gone.

The rumours arrived well before the official news. On September 17, 1941, Stalin finally gave permission to General Kirponov, head of the Soviet 5th Army, to withdraw from Kyiv. Once the orders went out to withdraw behind the Dnipro River, the Germans pounced and took control of the city in less than twenty-four hours.

But the withdrawal order had come too late. "Hurrying Heinz" Guderian, the great Panzer general, had already crossed the Dnipro in Belorussia in late August and had penetrated far east of the Ukrainian capital, to the area around Romny. General Ewald von Kleist blasted past the Dnipro south of Kyiv by September 10. On the September 14, the two generals shook hands a hundred miles east of Kyiv—having trapped five Soviet armies, more than half a million men, in the huge pocket between their forces.

It had not been the first time, nor would it be the last. The Soviet 6th and 12th armies had been encircled and trapped near Uman in mid-August. And after the Wehrmacht's capture of Minsk in July, they had captured another five Soviet armies.

General Kirponos had fought hard against the

encirclement in September, but a landmine killed him. Only a few in his army managed to break out.

Part of the 38th Army under newly appointed Major-General Vladimir Tsiganov managed to escape the Kyiv encirclement. Maurice and his men joined the retreat, heading southeast to defend the bridgeheads between Cherkassy and Kremenchuk. The Germans sent more Panzer divisions, and in October, the remnants of the Red Army pulled back another one hundred kilometres. Soldiers dug into the eastern banks of the shallow Psyol River to protect Poltava, where Marshall Timoshenko had his headquarters.

Maurice's unit took shelter in trenches built by the locals, but there were no bunkers this time. Food delivery became sporadic and the men griped continually about the autumn rain. The soft soil of the trench walls crumbled. The food was bad or there wasn't enough. But they could not complain for long. The Panzers kept coming.

They stayed awake all night, squinting west across the Psyol River to the invisible, continuous rumble of heavy vehicles. Some of the men prayed. Commissars and officers moved up and down the lines, inspecting and admonishing the soldiers to vigilance and readiness. "At the first sign of the Germans, we counterattack," they said.

Maurice doubted it.

That first sign came at dawn. As the sky greyed behind the Soviets, the early light picked out German tanks advancing along the roads, cautious yet swift.

Maurice's fingers tingled as the rising sun revealed columns of armoured vehicles and marching men, officers' staff cars and motorized cannons. The lines stretched for miles. The German army moved in unison, fast, alert and fearless like a predator.

Two Panzers ventured onto a small wooden bridge. They weren't even fazed when the bridge collapsed under their weight. The water didn't reach over the tops of their treads. The drivers down-shifted and continued on.

An officer shouted to Maurice's right and anti-tank guns fired. Shells burst on the lead Panzer and flames erupted around the turret, but didn't damage the tank. Its machine gun fired and then its cannon barked. Maurice saw Red soldiers' bodies fling up out of destroyed trenches.

"Fire!" Andrei and Orest pulled their triggers and the kick-back of the rifles geysered dirt into the air. *Damn,* Maurice thought. *If that doesn't draw the Germans' attention, nothing will.*

The shells went wide.

"Reload."

Machine guns erupted from behind and a German armoured car carrying dozens of soldiers exploded, throwing bodies high into the air.

Maurice's men fired again, and this time one shell hit a tank front-on. The shell stuck, burned into the metal plate and burst, but did not penetrate the armour. The tank reversed gears and drew back from the riverbank. The Panzers halted on the west bank, waiting.

All at once, shells began falling behind the Soviet lines, bursting and burning among the men. The Germans had turned their heavy artillery guns on the Red Army.

"Down, boys," Maurice said, pulling his helmet as low as he could. *It's hopeless. If a shell doesn't land in this trench and kill us all, it'll only be sheer luck.*

Soviet guns answered, sporadic and uncoordinated. They were aimed generally westward, in contrast to the German shells, which seemed demonically guided to Red Army targets.

When the heavy fire relented, Maurice chanced a look over the trench. The German tanks were advancing again. Somewhere, a heavy anti-tank gun fired, hitting the lead Panzer square on. The explosion blew its treads off and it lurched sideways into the river, crippled, smoke pouring from its front plate.

But more Panzers splashed through the river. Behind

them came soldiers, running from cover to cover, firing their fast submachine guns. As they climbed onto the near bank, some hit landmines and fell, crippled, but more Panzers drove around them.

To his right, eastward, came a deep rumble. Maurice saw hulking Soviet KV heavy tanks, looking twice as high as a man, crawled forward on their wide treads, firing cannons and machine guns.

Why are they moving so slowly, he wondered. He saw their tracks moving, churning the earth and sinking into it. *They're too heavy for the soft ground.* They were impervious to enemy fire unless it was point-blank on, but they were soon immobile. The Panzers just went around them.

"Pull back," Maurice yelled, and the boys picked up the guns and ammunition and ran, crouching low as they could to the next trench, where they joined several other odalenje. Maurice's boys hurriedly set up the guns and aimed at the Panzers.

They were too late.

The tanks swept past them, crushing wounded men under their treads. Andrei and Nikolai swung their gun around. "Aim at its back," Maurice said. "FIRE!"

The gun whooshed and the shell hit the Panzer's cylindrical fuel tank, oddly exposed on its rear deck behind the turret. The tank's rear end lifted high and Maurice thought it would flip over. Shards of metal flew in every direction and the tank's hull split and burned. The explosion rang in Maurice's ears for minutes.

"Let's get them, Lieutenant," Orest said. He stood to pick up the gun, and Viktor, his loader, looked at Maurice wide-eyed. "We killed one tank. Let's get more of the bastards."

Big Eugene stood too, submachine gun at the ready. "Get down," Maurice said. He grabbed Orest's uniform and pulled him to the ground. Big Eugene dropped as a shell burst thirty metres away. Maurice saw him crawl back to the trench, flat on his belly.

The Panzers halted and the Soviet infantry charged, advancing in a line and shooting as they ran. German machine guns cut them down by the dozen.

One Red soldier, bent almost double with rifle held low, ran across the field from the opposite side. Maurice marvelled the Germans did not notice him. He got to the closest Panzer and leapt onto its deck. Without breaking stride, he jammed a grenade under the turret and leapt off again, running and diving onto the ground. Maurice watched the explosion tear off the turret. Two Germans climbed out of the remains of the tank and fell to Soviet fire.

Smoke filled the battlefield, from explosions and gunfire, burning tanks, cars and trucks, trees and grass. Behind the black clouds, the sun rose red. Maurice could no longer see the brave Russian grenadier.

Another wave of Red soldiers charged forward and was cut down in turn. A third wave came forward, tripping over the corpses of their comrades. Time after time, the Red Army charged, men with obsolete rifles against the unmatched German machine guns that fired rounds at triple the rate of the Soviet models.

Only then did Maurice realize how much faster the German guns were. While the Soviet heavy machine guns chattered, the sound of the Germans' was an almost continuous buzz, like a hornet.

"Rifles ready, boys," he said, but he wouldn't order them to charge before he absolutely had to. *Let the commissar threaten me with a pistol, first.*

Soldiers fell like wheat before invisible scythes. But they kept charging. A few stopped for a moment to fling grenades or Molotov cocktails, which burst and flamed on the Panzers. It didn't look like much, but gasoline burning on the outer armour makes the inside of the tank too hot to tolerate. The crews threw open the hatches and tried to escape, dying as Maurice's men emptied their magazines.

Panzer machine guns strafed the Soviet lines. Then the

German infantry arrived, charging across the Psyol River on foot or on speedy armoured cars. The soldiers hid behind anything they could find, fired to cover their comrades ahead or behind them, leapfrogging toward the Soviet lines. They jumped into the first line of trenches the Soviets had abandoned minutes earlier and set up machine guns to add to the fire.

That was when the Cossacks charged. It was like something out of a movie. Men on horses, capes flapping behind them, swung curved sabres or fired machine guns. When they reached the German infantry, they slashed them, killing until they tumbled over their horses' necks as the invaders shot the mounts dead, or until fire blew the horsemen out of their saddles.

"Fire whenever you have them in your sights," Maurice said to the gunners. The corporals fired as quickly as the loaders could put ammunition in the breaches, and then ducked low as they became the focus of German machine-gun fire.

A commissar appeared among them and ordered a unit of riflemen to Maurice's right to charge the Germans. Maurice saw the fear on the faces of the soldiers. None of them were even twenty years old. They cradled their rifles and stared wide-eyed at the carnage on the fields.

An officer ordered "Charge!" and they scrambled over the lip of the trench. Maurice watched as boy after boy was hit by bullets and shrapnel. They clustered together, firing sporadically at anything that moved until a shell—German or Soviet, it was impossible to say—burst in their midst, killing at least six at once, including their sergeant.

Beyond them, Maurice could see a group of German soldiers creeping through the smoke. They lay on the ground, crawling on their bellies, until they stopped in a line, guns aimed at the odalenje that had climbed out of the trench.

Another German group crept closer just beyond the first, aiming their submachine guns, then halted until the first group crept past them. Alternately, they crawled closer and closer to the Soviet lines.

"Aim your rifles at Fritz over there," Maurice said. But the Soviet unit ordered to charge was between them and the enemy. They crouched, stupidly, in the middle of the field, exposed to fire from all sides. While some fired their rifles occasionally, the rest appeared frozen. They had no idea what to do, and they didn't see the enemy crawling toward them.

Someone shouted behind Maurice. A sergeant at a machine gun was trying to communicate with the young soldiers. "Get down. Get out of the way. You're blocking my fire, you idiots."

But the boys could not hear him over the roar of battle. Even if they had, Maurice doubted whether they'd have known where to go without their commander. "*Get down*," the soldier yelled again. It was futile.

Maurice tried. "Get back to the trench." But they remained where they were, shooting occasionally, frozen with fear. One by one, they caught bullets and fell, sometimes screaming.

The Germans kept coming and Maurice then saw their objective: a big M-45 anti-tank gun firing as fast as its crew could reload. It had been placed too close to the front line, and as the infantry had fallen back from the first trench to the second, it had been stranded. Still, it was taking a toll on the Panzers and armoured cars, and this group of German soldiers had been ordered to take it out. As they moved closer to the gun, the stranded group of Russian boys became ever more directly between them and the Soviet guns.

The sergeant behind Maurice screamed frantically at the boys to get out of the way. Maurice and all his men yelled too, but it was no use. Then two of the Germans raised themselves just enough to throw grenades.

Pop-pop-pop-pop. The machine gun behind Maurice fired. Bullets ripped up the grass between him and the crawling

Germans, and one fell forward with a grenade in his hand. Seconds later, the incendiary exploded and he disappeared in a cloud of smoke and soil. The second grenadier flattened himself on the ground then twisted as the bullets tore into his body.

The remaining Germans turned their fire toward the machine gun, and incidentally on the company of young soldiers between them. Sick to his stomach, Maurice could only watch as fire from both sides tore the young men to pieces. He knew the machine gun sergeant could not wait anymore—saving the anti-tank gun meant saving a lot more lives than one odalenje which, exposed to fire from all sides, was fated to be cut down sooner or later.

In moments, the whole platoon lay dead, scattered on the ground like rag dolls. The battle continued around their bodies.

Without their comrades in the way, Maurice's boys started shooting at the remaining German company. Orest and Viktor fired an antipersonnel shell that ripped the survivors to pieces. For a moment, Maurice let himself fantasize they might win this battle. Then he heard another roar and he realized the Panzers were moving again.

A commissar dropped into the trench, followed by two NKVD men in their distinctive green caps. "Fall back, comrade," he said. "Regroup in the village." He moved along the trench to the next platoon, ordering them to stay behind as a rear guard.

Both the commissar and the men he ordered knew it was a death sentence. The NKVD men were there to ensure they didn't break and run. They knew it was a suicide mission for them, too.

Maurice's boys took the guns apart, picked up the ammunition and scurried along a connecting trench to the next set of fortifications, and from there farther from the battle. Eventually, they reached the half-destroyed village, where most of the buildings were burning.

"Don't leave anything behind," an officer said. "Load

the weapons onto wagons." By noon, Maurice and his boys trudged through fields of high grain. Behind them, smoke billowed into the sky as the last Soviet defenders gave their lives to cover their comrades' retreat.

Chapter 11: The bootless army

Eastern Ukraine, October, 1941

By autumn 1941, the Red Army was exhausted, filthy and covered in lice. Maurice had been wearing the same uniform for weeks, since his regiment had slipped through the German encirclement east of the Psyol River.

One word characterized the Red Army in 1941: retreat. By September, they were down to half-rations. The regiments had to steal water from the farms they were supposed to be defending. Soldiers' boots fell apart after hundreds of kilometres of retreating across thick mud that threatened to swallow men whole. Divisions ran out of ammunition every day, and the army could not replace damaged uniforms.

While the officers had sturdy leather boots, the enlisted men's boots were leather only on the lower section. The uppers were felt, which shredded quickly. By fall, the boots fell apart, and Maurice saw men wrap their feet in newspapers.

Newspapers filled with propaganda about how we're beating the Germans back. Wrapping feet is all they're good for.

Even Sergeant Petro's ability to scrounge provisions reached its limit by mid-September. The boys sewed up tears in their clothing as best they could, but their ragged uniforms made them look more like beggars than an army. Even Maurice's boots leaked.

Germany's invasion of the Soviet Union had been on a scale the world had never seen. Millions of men, hundreds of thousands of tanks and trucks and airplanes swept across the plains of eastern Poland, Ukraine and Belorussia, and then into Russia itself. Outgunned, undertrained, lacking almost everything except sheer numbers of men, the Red Army retreated until they were surrounded and destroyed or captured. The Germans boasted about capturing whole armies, hundreds of thousands of men.

Most prisoners did not survive until the end of the war.

The Red Army's ferocity in retreat became legendary. Especially in Ukraine, where the Soviets fought with a bravery and savagery out of proportion to their equipment, organization and leadership. Soldiers would hide under stacks of hay while the invaders swept past. Knowing they had been abandoned by their units, they would attack the Germans' rear, killing scores before they were cut down.

Maurice focused on keeping his "boys" alive. By day, they hid as best they could in stands of trees, behind burned-down farm buildings or in ditches. At night, they gathered the guns, ammunition and their personal equipment. The boys would take turns pulling a wagon while Maurice fended off the senior officers' urges to gather with the rest of the army. Maurice knew that would only make them a bigger target.

Instead, the boys would find an abandoned barn or shed. The officers would have one soldier shoot a pig or a cow, and the men would eat for a night. But most of the time they retreated, walking if not running east just to stay ahead of the Germans.

One afternoon in September, a mounted major rode up to Maurice. The horse looked as worn as Maurice felt. It head hung low, its tail drooped. The saddle was tattered and broken, and the major riding it did not look much better.

"We're ten miles from Kharkiv," he said, his voice dry and scratchy. "There's a forest two miles north of here. We'll take refuge there for the rest of the day."

"I have orders to go south and dig in for Fritz," Maurice lied.

"No arguments, soldier." The major sat up straight in his saddle, one hand settling on the hilt of his sabre. "I want your unit to fall in with the rest of us within the hour. If I don't see you there, I'll shoot you myself."

Maurice saluted as ironically as he could. The major slumped again as the horse shuffled off to the next unit to pass on the same order.

The same stupid order, Maurice thought.

Maurice led his boys behind a stream of Red Army units down a forest path worn and widened by thousands of men. Most of the enlisted men were barefoot, their felt boots worn away. Even the officers' uniforms were tattered. Men, not horses, pushed or pulled wagons or dragged crates of ammunition behind them.

After a half-hour, the forest opened to a wide glade filled with the Red Army. Men collapsed into the tall grass, dropping their weapons on the ground without bothering to stack them. No fires burned. There was no food to eat.

Maurice led his odalenye to a clear spot near the edge of the forest. "Stack your rifles, boys." They stacked them in a circle and arranged the parts of the anti-tank guns beside them. Then they collapsed like the rest.

"Think we're safe here?" Orest asked.

"Safe as anywhere from Fritz," Yuri said.

"Are we safe from the Russians?" another private—Slawko—said in a low voice Maurice could barely hear. "We could slip into the woods, hide until Fritz goes past us, then sneak back home."

"Quiet," Maurice said, hissing. "The commissars hear everything." He looked over each shoulder, but didn't see

Matvienko or any of the other political officers. For that matter, he couldn't spot another officer in the clearing. Where was the major on his worn-out nag?

"Why do you worry about the Russians?" Slawko said. "Stalin ordered scorched earth. We had to burn our own homes down."

"It's the same all over Russia," Orest said.

"We burned down farms in Ukraine," Slawko said. "Not in Russia. And Stalin's Georgian. What does he care about Ukraine?"

Maurice leaned into the circle of men. "If a commissar hears even a whisper about desertion," he said as loudly as he dared, "he'll shoot all of us without hesitation."

Slawko's eyes darted to every man in the odalenye before he slumped back into the grass. Maurice let out a breath he hadn't realized he had been holding. Then he heard a rumble. He turned just in time to hear four men yell at once. "Halt."

All around the perimeter of the clearing, men wearing grey uniforms and holding submachine guns stepped out of the woods.

They were captured.

A captain stepped forward, pistol in hand. Two machine gun-bearing corporals stepped ahead with him. "Politruk (political commissar)," he called. The Red Army men did not respond.

Why do they want the commissars? Maurice wondered. He started to feel sick to his stomach.

"Politruck," the German captain called again. "Step forward." Still, no one moved. The officer motioned with his gun, and three German soldiers stepped forward and walked among the Red Army men. One by one, they grabbed political officers and lined them up in front of their captain.

When the German soldiers could not find any more commissars, they saluted their commander and stood to one side. Six young officers, each wearing the insignia of the political wing on their collars, stood before the German captain. Maurice did not see Matvienko among them.

"Kneel," he said to the commissars. But they did not understand German. They only looked at one another.

Maurice felt his throat go dry.

German soldiers stepped forward and pushed the commissars to their knees. The officer strutted back and forth, as if he were inspecting them. At the end of the line, he looked at his own men and said, in German, "They're pathetic." He stepped behind the last commissar, raised his gun to the man's head and pulled the trigger.

The sound of the gunshot hit Maurice like a slap in the face. Even after all the death he had seen since Kyiv, he shook when he saw the commissar's body fall to the ground.

The German officer stepped behind the line of commissars and shot them one by one. When six bodies lay on the ground, he holstered his weapon and looked up at a sergeant major. "March them to Kharkiv."

The Germans rode in armoured cars, the officers on horses, but the Soviet soldiers marched or limped along the cratered road to Kharkiv. More German soldiers, some with submachine guns, some with rifles, lined the street in the city. No one thought of escaping.

They walked into a big, square room made of fitted stones in the seventeenth-century fortress in the middle of the city. No beds, no cots, no bunks. The prisoners collapsed to sleep on the bare floor.

The smell would have made Maurice retch if he had eaten anything in the past twelve hours. He looked at his men and saw nothing but despair.

"Put all our gear together here," Maurice said. "We'll sleep in a circle, heads together, around our things. That way, no one will be able to steal it when we're asleep."

The boys piled what little the Germans had let them

keep—gloves, a few changes of underwear, odd personal things—then arranged themselves around them like spokes of a wheel. Maurice added his torn pack, but kept his shenil, his greatcoat, as a blanket. His one treasure, his Dominion of Canada birth certificate, was in an inner pocket, next to his skin.

He lay awake, staring up into pitch blackness. He had never felt so afraid of dying before, not even when the shells were exploding overhead and the Panzers were racing across streams and tearing up grain fields before his eyes. He felt sure if he closed his eyes, he would never open them again.

Unwelcome sleep came, blessing him with a short oblivion.

The Germans woke them before dawn, not with bugles but with SS soldiers carrying submachine guns. They strode across the stone room, screaming "*Raus! Raus*! Out, you fuckers. Get off your arses, you animals."

They staggered out, without any belongings. A German private gave each man a small piece of bread. They lined up for a cup of water, and then they were each given a hammer, pick or barrow and marched out the gate for a day of breaking rocks.

Within a week, Maurice's uniform was tattered, stinking, stiff, caked with dirt and cordite. Lice crawled on his scalp and the shrapnel scar on his left knee ached. His hands stung from breaking rocks into gravel for the Germans to make new roads. The only thing that kept him from weeping was knowing his men, and the hundreds of thousands of other Red Army conscripts around him, suffered even more from starvation rations, cold and forced labour. Starving and exhausted, they had no energy, privacy nor time to even dream of escape.

Maurice dropped his sledgehammer and joined the line-up for supper. The sun was already down and the air was chill. No one had the energy to complain. They shuffled ahead to where a German private ladled soup from a barrel into small metal bowls. Fish heads floating in water, that's what the Germans called soup for the prisoners on the eastern front.

When the prisoners staggered back to the camp the next day, Maurice could barely hold onto his sledgehammer. Supper was more generous, a piece of dry bread, another bowl of soup, but this time it was a little thicker, with a piece of strange-tasting meat. Maurice wondered about that. It was tough and tasted bad, but he ate it. That night, he had no trouble falling asleep.

He learned about the meat a week later. That morning, as they ate their miserable breakfast, a Russian corporal who had been given a few extra rations by the Germans in return for his service as an interpreter called out three names. "Bury, Shemko, Rossoviski. Come with me."

The three listless men followed the corporal to a truck and climbed in the back, joining five others. As he closed the door, the corporal smiled at them. "You're lucky. You're on meat duty today."

One of the other men in the truck groaned. As the truck lurched toward the gates, Maurice looked at him with a question on his face.

"You wonder where our meat ration comes from? We're going to get it."

"What kind of meat?" Maurice dreaded the answer.

"Horsemeat, of course."

"I don't understand."

"You will."

An hour later, the truck lurched to a halt. When the guards opened the back doors, the eight prisoners nearly fell out and found themselves at the front lines again—or rather, where the front lines had been the day before.

The landscape was dead. Nothing green was in sight. Smoke hung in the air and the men could hear the noise of battle, the boom of cannon and guns far off. Scattered in every direction as far as the men could see were remains of shattered buildings and trees and cars and tanks and other machines. Broken rifles and guns, shell casings and helmets.

"All right, get to work, Slavs," a German sergeant said, and the men moved across the battlefield. The guards with sub-machine guns watched carefully.

The dead soldiers had already been taken away, but the ground was still littered with the bodies of horses and other animals. Both the Red Army and the Wehrmacht used horses to pull ammunition and guns. Horses had the advantage of not sinking into the deep, rich black earth of Ukraine—unlike tanks.

Four men moved to a dead horse, lying with its legs and neck twisted around a large rock. Maurice saw bullet holes through its neck and chest. He didn't look closely anymore. The men struggled to drag the animal to the truck. There, they used big butcher knives to hack the body into manageable chunks, loaded it into bins, then hoisted them into the back of another truck. Then they went back into the field for some more.

Maurice was pulling the head of a horse toward a trench they had dug when he heard the Germans shouting. He looked up to see three soldiers aiming their rifles in the same direction. The sergeant shouted, "Halt!" while a corporal blew a whistle.

Maurice turned. Across the field, a prisoner ran for the tree line.

"Halt," the sergeant called again. The soldiers with rifles were looking at him, and he nodded once. The soldiers squinted down their barrels and three shots sounded like one.

Maurice could not breathe. He turned again toward the trees and for a second thought, *He made it. He got away.* Then he saw another body splayed on the ground.

"Got him," one of the soldiers said, grinning at his fellows.

"No you didn't. I got him," said another, a skinny man

who could not have been more than seventeen.

Beside Maurice, another prisoner threw up a thin stream of liquid, almost pure water. There was nothing in his stomach to expel.

"You couldn't hit a barn, Ansel," the first soldier said. "You're a lousy shot."

"That's not true," skinny Ansel said. "I'm just as good as you are."

"Oh yeah? Shoot him again."

Ansel raised his rifle to his shoulder. "He's lying down, now. Not much of a target." He fired, but no one could see where the bullet went.

The first soldier laughed and shook his head. He raised his rifle, squinted down the barrel and squeezed the trigger. Maurice saw the body, thirty metres away, twitch. For the briefest moment, he wondered if the prisoner still lived.

"Better than me, eh, Ansel," the soldier said, grinning.

"Stop wasting ammunition," a corporal said. "And you, prisoners, get back to work." He pointed to another prisoner. "You, go dig a hole and put that man in it. And if you try anything, you and your friend here," he nodded toward Maurice, "will join him. Got it?"

The prisoner, a thin man with a dirty cloth bandage wrapped around one arm, did not understand. He stared with his mouth open at the soldier who had shot the escapee, until the corporal got angry and brandished his rifle. "Are you deaf? You want a bullet, too?"

Maurice spoke in Russian. "He wants you to bury that man." The thin prisoner's eyes shifted from the German corporal to Maurice without changing expression. Maurice took his elbow. "Come on, I'll help you." They stepped toward the dead man.

"Did I tell you to help?" the corporal asked. "Get back to what you were doing, or your friend will have two bodies to bury."

"He wants you to do it yourself," Maurice said. He picked up the horse head again and lugged it to the trench, not daring to look up at anyone. From the corner of his eye, he could see the thin Russian limp to his comrade's body, struggle to break the packed, cold ground, and eventually push the body into a hole.

Hours later, the prisoners were covered in horse blood, gore and filth. They somehow pulled themselves back up into the truck and rode to the camp. No one said a word. They unloaded the meat bins near the kitchen and were marched back to their quarters. Uniform and all, they walked into an improvised outdoor shower. The German guards turned on a strong blast of freezing water. The prisoner shivered and moaned, but they were glad to rinse off at least some of the filth.

Maurice could not eat that evening, but later went to the kitchen to talk to the cook. A guard watched him cross the camp, eyes narrow, puffing on his cigarette.

The cook was another prisoner, Kuzenko. He was cleaning up and gave Maurice a piece of bread.

"I didn't know the horsemeat came from the battlefield," Maurice said.

"It's more efficient. Why waste anything? The Germans hate to waste," Kuzenko said. "Besides, horse is cleaner than cow."

"How clean can it be, coming from a battlefield?"

"We steam it, so you won't get diarrhea. And if you get a good piece, it's good meat. Once you get used to the taste."

Maurice got used to eating it within days. Tastes and standards have a way of slipping when you're starving.

Maurice knew neither he nor any of his men could survive long in the POW camp. They were all weak with hunger. A minor infection, even a cold, could kill all of them. He did what he could to buy them as much rest as possible, but there wasn't much latitude. And the Germans never showed a bit of mercy.

He would learn years later, long after the war, that the

Germans treated their Slavic prisoners differently from those of the Western Allies. Soviet prisoners were forced to work, and they got half the food the Westerners did—starvation rations for the *untermensch*, the sub-human Slavs. More than twice as many Soviet soldiers died in captivity.

After a few weeks, Maurice knew he and his men had little time left. They were so weak, they could barely rise from the floor in the morning. Often, Maurice would feel dizzy just walking across the compound. He knew the other prisoners felt the same. Two or three committed suicide every day, hanging themselves with their belts or provoking the guards to shoot them.

One October evening, Maurice picked up an empty bottle rolling across the courtyard of the old fortress. Its smooth surface was strangely comforting under his fingers. He briefly thought about breaking it to cut a German, but knew he would be shot within seconds.

He thought of his mother and sister on the farm in Ternopyl. *I have to get out of here. I have to get back to them.*

He looked up at German soldiers in gun towers, patrolling along the ancient walls. He shook his head.

Inspired, he sat on the ground and brushed dirt off a small area of the cobblestones, took off his shirt and spread it on the clear spot. He rolled the bottle over his shirt. The crunching of the lice under the bottle felt satisfying—the best feeling he had in months.

The effort exhausted him. He slumped back, leaning against the barracks behind him. He saw men in grey uniforms marching and walking across the courtyard. One, a young man with light brown hair and hazel eyes, came toward him with a puzzled expression on his face.

Maurice focused on that face and saw a miracle.

The young man wore a German officer's uniform, impeccably pressed. He frowned, tilted his head and stepped back. He began to turn away, but stopped and looked closer.

"Maurice?" he said. "Is it you?"

Chapter 12: Daniel

Kharkiv, November, 1941

"Stand up, prisoner."

Maurice looked up to see a young German private in front of him, rifle slung over his shoulder. Bohdan, now a captain in the German army, stood behind him.

Maurice pulled his tattered jacket over his grimy shirt, wishing he hadn't broken the bottle he had been using to crush lice the night before. His hat was long gone. *How long have I been sitting here?* he wondered. The sun was low over the buildings of the old fortress, the shadows long.

"Come with me, prisoner," Bohdan said, and walked across the courtyard. Maurice hesitated until the German private shoved his shoulder. "Get moving."

Maurice stumbled after his old friend, conscious of the soldier behind him, wondering if he had unslung his rifle. They were walking toward the main gate of the old fortress, where an open, four-wheel-drive vehicle waited with a driver behind the wheel.

The soldier behind Maurice gestured for him to get into the back of the vehicle while Bohdan stepped to the guard at the gate and showed him a slip of paper. Maurice heard him say in German, "I'm taking this prisoner for special interrogation." The guard grinned, nodded at another guard and the gate swung open. Bohdan climbed into the front passenger seat, the soldier beside Maurice in the back, and the car moved to the gate.

Maurice could not believe what was happening. As it drew even with the gate guardhouse, he thought the guards would pull him out of the car. His body tensed, anticipating a rifle butt in the back or shoulder. But the guards nodded at Bohdan as the car eased past, and then they were out of the fortress, driving into the blacked-out streets of Kharkiv.

Other than an occasional German army truck or a staff car, there was no traffic. Bohdan directed the driver street by street, telling him to turn left here, right there, but never providing an address.

When did he learn his way around Kharkiv? Maurice wondered.

Every wall seemed to have been cracked or pockmarked with bullet holes. Bricks and pieces of walls lay on the ground, strewn across the streets. Shops, factories and houses had collapsed, crushed and bombed out. The street itself was cracked and holed, and the driver had to swerve continually around craters.

Even with the damage though, Maurice could see they had come to a wealthy residential area of the city. Big houses stood behind stone walls, looking grand even though most of the walls were damaged or outright broken.

The car stopped in front of a large house. A stone wall as high as Maurice's head had once surrounded it, but it had collapsed along the street. Piles of broken bricks and stone choked most of the street. Even in the early evening gloom, Maurice could see the garden had been hit with at least one bomb. The house itself, however, appeared undamaged, though all its windows were dark.

Maurice, Bohdan and the soldier got climbed out of the car and stepped up to the grand door, which had been painted red. The soldier rapped on the door. "Open," he said. The door swung back immediately, revealing luxuries

Maurice had forgotten existed—lights, carpets, painted walls, civilization.

Bohdan pulled Maurice inside with him and shut the door quickly so he would not break the blackout rules. The soldier remained outside.

A short, dark man in an expensive suit stood in front of them. "Good evening, Herr Joachim," Bohdan said. "Maurice, this is my friend, Mr. Joachim. Joachim, Maurice Bury, my oldest friend from college. I want you to take good care of him tonight."

The short man said nothing, but led them down a dark wood-paneled hall into his study. One wall was covered floor to ceiling with bookshelves. A desk with an electric lamp sat at one end of the room, and at the other were three cushioned chairs. Mr. Joachim sat in one and held his hand out to indicate they should sit, too.

Despite his fatigue, Maurice could not relax. He perched on the edge of the seat, conscious of the filth ground into his clothes, his skin and his hair. He hoped he did not smudge or stain the upholstery or the soft rug under his worn-out boots.

"I'll be back in the morning, Joachim," Bohdan said. "Give Maurice a bath, something to eat, a bed and clean clothes in the morning." The short man nodded, still silent.

"Aren't you taking an awful chance, Bohdan? What if he reports you?" Maurice said.

Bohdan smiled. "He won't report me, because I will not report him."

"For what?"

"For being a Jew."

Maurice looked around the room. There was no sign the owner was Jewish—no menorah, no stars. "He's hiding that he's Jewish?"

Joachim spoke for the first time. "I have a family to protect."

"I'll be back in the morning, Maurice, and I'll send you

home," Bohdan said.

"What about my men?"

"What about them?"

"You have to get them out, too," Maurice said.

One part of Maurice was amazed he pushed his luck like this, but he knew he had no choice. He had to help his men get out of the fortress.

"Are you crazy? I got you out, at considerable risk already, Maurice. If the colonel finds out…"

"You'll be shot. I know. But you'll be shot whether you free one man or twelve, or one hundred. I've kept these boys alive through this war, Bohdan. I promised they would return home."

"That's a meaningless promise in wartime, Maurice. You know I can't take twelve men out of the camp. You're my friend, but your men...well, they're just soldiers. I can't convince the commandant to let them go."

"Didn't you convince him to let me go?"

Anger flashed across Bohdan's face. "He doesn't know you're gone. And now, no one knows you were ever there. You were never captured, Maurice. Do you get it now? You died on the battlefield."

Maurice swayed in the chair. He closed his eyes and nearly fell off his seat before Bohdan pushed him upright again. Maurice took a deep breath and tried to focus on his friend's face. "You have to get them out. Eleven men, my odalenye."

Bohdan sighed and stood. "I'll do what I can, Maurice. But I cannot make any promises." He nodded to Joachim and left without another word.

Maurice and Joachim looked at each other for a minute, and Maurice again realized how dirty he was.

Apparently, so did Mr. Joachim. "Come with me," he said, and led him to a bathroom at the back of the house. "You had better clean up as best you can. I will have the girl bring some towels and a nightshirt. Just don't use up all the water. We're being rationed. Jews get less than goyim."

When Joachim closed the bathroom door behind him, Maurice was alone for the first time in months. It was a strange feeling, not to be conscious of others around him, to be able to undress without hesitating. He poured a few centimetres of tepid water into the tub and stepped in.

This is so much nicer, so much more luxurious than my mother's bathroom.

Washing turned the water dark grey almost immediately. He emptied the tub and, feeling a little guilty, poured another few centimetres in. *He's a rich Jew. He can afford a little extra hot water. Besides, I'm still dirty.*

This time, the water did not look as horrible after he finished. He found a comb beside the sink and leaned over the tub to comb lice out of his hair, then rinsed them down the drain with as little water as he could. It was the first time he had been clean in months, the lice notwithstanding.

He heard a knock at the door and the young maid's voice. "Mr. Soldier? I have a night shirt for you." He stood behind the door and opened it just enough for the maid's arm, and took the white nightshirt.

Pulling it on made him feel transformed. He knew he was still dirty, starving and sick. But now, he almost felt normal again. No longer a soldier, an officer, just a man who had the ability and the inclination to care about his own appearance.

He went back to the kitchen, bare feet slapping on the floor. Joachim waited there for him, folding his newspaper as Maurice came in. He stood and without speaking, led him upstairs to a small bedroom. From the lack of decorations or personal items, Maurice could see it was a guest room.

"Goodnight, Mr. Bury. And when you return home, try to think kindly of a Jewish family who helped you."

Despite his exhaustion, hunger and anxiety kept Maurice awake for hours. He kept imagining German soldiers bursting into the house, dragging him, Joachim and the little blond maid into the street and shooting them all in the head.

Outside the window, no light shone. The Germans had imposed a blackout for fear of Soviet air attacks and a strict curfew on the local population for fear of insurrection. Maurice stretched out on the bed.

The last time I saw Bohdan was in a bar in Poland three years ago.

Chapter 13: Crackdown

Peremyshl, Poland, 1938

Bohdan took off his student uniform jacket and draped it on the back of chair, then went to the bar as Maurice sat down. He brought back two tall glasses and set one in front of Maurice. "German beer," he said. "It's what everybody's drinking these days."

"Pah. What do the Germans know?" said a young man at the table beside them. A student, but to judge by his clothes he was from a farm like Maurice. "Give me good Ukrainian vodka any day."

"You've already had more than enough vodka, Roman," a young man in a cloth cap said, laughing. Roman glared at him but slumped back in his chair, silent.

The dance hall was the dirtiest building Maurice had ever seen, except for a barn. *No, this place is worse than my mother's barn. The cats get rid of the mice in my mother's barn.*

The walls had holes and the middle of the dance floor warped upward. Every window was covered with plywood. Catering to Ukrainians, the dance hall could only open secretly after dark, in hopes the Polish authorities would not notice. New laws had imposed a night time curfew, shut down Ukrainian cultural centres and forbidden speaking Ukrainian in government establishments.

The band played an old Ukrainian tune and

somewhere, someone sang along. It was still early and people were not drunk enough yet to feel like joining in.

"The Germans have the right idea, whether you like their beer or not," another young man said. Maurice recognized him as a senior student from the gymnasium and thought his name was Danylo, but couldn't be certain. He had spread three newspapers across their table, one in Polish, one in German and the last in Russian. He had been comparing coverage among the three when Bohdan and Maurice had arrived. "You have to admit, Hitler has made Germany strong again," he said, pointing to the newspapers.

"Too strong, too fast, if you ask me," the man in the cloth cap said.

Maurice looked at a table beside the opposite wall where a group of young women chatted, sipped vodka and nodded to the music. A pretty dark-haired woman caught his eye, smiled and turned away.

"The stronger Germany gets, the worse for Poland," the man in the cap said.

"There's a likely bunch," Bohdan said, nodding toward the women. They saw the pretty dark-haired woman lean close to her girlfriend. She said something, the girlfriend glanced at Maurice and Bohdan, and both women laughed.

Maurice stood, picking up his beer. "Come on. Let's meet the girls." He smiled at the brunette as he crossed the room, and she smiled back.

"Hi. My friend, here," he tossed his head back without checking to see whether Bohdan was behind him, "is shy, so he wants you to introduce him to your friend."

Bohdan remained quiet.

"I'm Oksana," the dark-haired woman said, holding out her hand. Maurice shook it gently. She turned to the short, blond woman beside her. "This is Irina. What's your friend's name?"

Bohdan stepped forward, smiling, and took Irina's hand. Before he or Maurice could say anything, the band launched into a fast Volyn tune. The other women at the table jumped up, took Oksana and Irina by the hands and began dancing in a circle.

Bohdan sighed. "I hate it when girls do that."

"No, it's good," Maurice said, watching the girls step and jump. Oksana's long, dark hair swirled around her shoulders and she laughed. "Just follow me." He danced up to the circle, took Oksana's hands and began a two-step, a modern dance he had seen once, but to the traditional music. Bohdan took Irina's hands a second later.

Oksana looked surprised, but not unhappy. Maurice smiled wider and looked in her bright blue eyes. She smiled back and followed across the dance floor.

The next song was a waltz the band copied from the radio. Maurice and Bohdan traded partners, then traded again for a third song. When it was over, Oksana insisted on sitting again. "You dance very well, but you did not tell me your name," she said as she led him back to her table.

"Maurice," he said. "But you look thirsty. Come on. Bohdan, help me get the girls something to drink." Reluctant to leave Irina's side, Bohdan followed Maurice to the bar.

"Why can't you just get a bottle yourself?" he asked.

"How much money do you have?"

"Enough for a bottle. Don't you?"

"Not enough for the whole table," Maurice said, asking the bartender for a pitcher of beer.

"Why are we buying booze for the whole table, and not just for Irina and Oksana?"

"Because girls don't want to leave out their friends," Maurice said. "You pay the barkeep and bring the glasses."

But by the time they returned to the girls' table with a pitcher of beer, eight glasses and a new bottle of vodka, the girls were getting up to dance together again. "We'll be back soon," Oksana said.

At the table beside the bar, Danylo, Roman and the

man in the cap were still arguing about Germany. "Hitler's got the right idea," Danylo said. "He puts the Germans first, makes Germany for Germans."

"Not so good for the Jews, though, is it?" the man in the cap said.

"Let the Jews look after the Jews," Roman said. "They look after themselves and don't give a shit about anyone else."

Cap-man nodded at Bohdan and Maurice. "What about you two? What do you think?"

"About the Jews?" Bohdan asked. He was still thinking about the girls at the next table.

"Let the Jews be," Maurice said. "Do you know any of those girls at that table?"

"The point is not the Jews," Danylo said. "We need to do the same thing here—have Ukraine for Ukrainians."

"That's hard to do with the Poles in charge," the man in the cap said. "They're making Poland for Poles."

"Well, Lviv should be for Ukrainians," Roman said. "Kick the Poles out of the whole of Lviv Oblast."

"Then what?" the man in the cap said. "Join Ukraine, under the Russians? Should we all starve to death?"

"No," Danylo said, leaning over the table and speaking lower. "We revive the People's Republic of West Ukraine. Only this time, we include Lviv, the whole oblast and none of that commie crap. A national state, like Germany."

Cap man laughed and shook his head. "West Ukraine? How long did that last—a year? Do you really think the Poles will tolerate that? Or the Soviets?"

The music ended as the band took a break, just in time for Roman to shout, "Fuck the Poles. Fuck the Russians. Fuck Stalin." Roman threw another shot of vodka down his throat.

"Shut up," Danylo said. "Do you want to get us all thrown out?" He leaned closer again. "I think we could get Hitler's support, especially if it destabilizes Poland."

So many choices, Maurice thought. He was about to say "Why hasn't anyone suggested a united Ukraine, independent of Russia, Poland or Germany?" But just as he opened his mouth, the young women returned to their table and one of them began pouring the pitcher of beer into glasses. Maurice nudged Bohdan and they sat with Oksana and Irina again.

"So, you're interested in politics?" Oksana asked, sipping beer.

"Sure," Maurice said. "You have to take an interest."

"We're patriots," Bohdan said. "What about you girls?"

Maurice offered cigarettes then lit them before giving one to Bohdan and lighting his own.

"Oh, we're not political," Irina said, but she kept glancing from Roman to Danylo and the man in the cap as they argued.

"We're just here for some fun, not for an argument." Oksana laughed and put her hand on Maurice's arm. Maurice took a deep drag on his cigarette and hoped his hands did not shake.

"That's what we're here for, too," Maurice said, smoke wreathing his head as he spoke. He hoped it would impress Oksana. "Right, Bohdan?"

"Absolutely," Bohdan shouted as the band struck up again. He took Irina's hands and pulled her onto the dance floor. Maurice took Oksana behind them.

Three more dances and Maurice took Oksana out a side door to cool down. He lit two more cigarettes and asked Oksana about herself.

"We're all from little towns around here, and we came to town to get jobs in the distillery," she said, flicking ash into the gutter.

"What's the distillery like?" he asked, wishing he could think of a better question.

Oksana shrugged. "Smelly. It's a job."

Maurice asked her about her family, back in the little

village. "It's me, my sisters and my mother," she said. "I'm the youngest."

"No father? Me, neither."

Oksana shrugged again and took another drag on her cigarette. "I never knew my father. He was killed in the Polish-Ukrainian war in 1920, before I was even born."

"I'm sorry," Maurice said.

She shrugged again. "Like I said, I never knew him. But I don't like Poles, much."

Maurice leaned closer until their lips met. Oksana kissed hard, intense and didn't break away for a long time. "So, student-boy, how late can you stay out tonight before you get into trouble?"

"I'm already way past curfew." He leaned in for another kiss. He could hear his pulse in his ears.

She pulled away again. "Get me another drink and then we can go," she said.

Maurice did not ask "where." He could not bring her to the school dormitory, so he hoped she meant her place. He pushed the open the side door to the dance hall just in time to see the front door crash inward and six policemen rush in. They carried clubs in their hands, and the leader brandished a pistol.

The band stopped with a shriek from an abused violin and every girl screamed.

"Everybody stand still," the lead policeman hollered in Polish. "Stop where you are this instant. You are all under arrest."

The barman came around his counter. "No one was making any trouble, sir," he said in Polish, hands out in supplication. "We're just having a good time. A little music, a little dancing..."

"What kind of music was the band playing?"

"You know, the hit parade, some traditional..."

"What language? Polish or Ukrainian?" He spat the last word out like it was dirty.

"Look at this, Jerzy," one of the cops said, pointing to

the table where Danylo had spread out his newspapers. Maurice saw a pamphlet beside the broadsheets and groaned when he saw the Cyrillic lettering. It was in Ukrainian.

Jerzy, the lead policeman, swept it up in his hand as if he had scored a point. “Sedition,” he said. “Arrest everyone.”

Roman launched himself at the nearest cop and landed a punch on his nose, which had almost no effect. The cop retaliated by hitting Roman on the head with his club, and Roman fell.

Then every man in the place began throwing punches. Maurice saw the man in the hat pull a club out of a cop’s hands. He hit the officer hard, knocking him down, and turned on a pair who were clubbing the barman.

Maurice could not see Bohdan. Oksana pulled on his arm. “Come on, don’t be stupid. Let’s get out of here.”

“But my friend—”

“You can’t help him. Come on.” Oksana hauled him out the side door, and Maurice had only a second to wonder how the cops could have been so stupid as to raid a dance hall without covering all the exits.

He ran behind Oksana down a dark alley and into another street, across two blocks, then more turns. Within minutes, he had no idea where they were.

The neighbourhood had few streetlights. Maurice could barely see Oksana as he stopped to catch his breath. Oksana looked up and down the alley. “No cops. Come on.” She pulled Maurice around a corner toward darker shadows.

“Where are we going?”

“My place. Don’t worry, it’s not far.”

“Aren’t you worried about your friends? Irina?”

“The cops won’t hold the girls. They might try to kiss or grope them, but they won’t hold them. Your friends, though, they’re in trouble if they don’t run.”

Maurice looked back the way they had come as if he

could see some of the others from the dance hall. "I wish I knew Bohdan was all right."

"He seemed pretty smart to me. I think he can look after himself."

She led him into a two-storey apartment building. He hesitated at the door. "I should get back to the dorm..."

"It's after curfew. Are you trying to get arrested?" Oksana pulled Maurice in, led him up the stairs and paused only to unlock the door to an apartment. Inside, she pulled his head down to kiss him, held his lips in hers and she pushed his jacket off.

When she let him go, she pulled him by the arm into a bedroom and unbuttoned her blouse. She started on his shirt buttons as Maurice bent to kiss her again.

He reached behind her and fumbled with her brassiere. Oksana laughed. "Oh, schoolboy, is this your first time?"

"No." He lied and finally managed to unhook her bra. He kissed her to silence her laughter and they fell onto the bed.

Later, Maurice kissed Oksana gently. "I have to go."

She pretended to pout. "Can't you stay at least until morning?"

"I have to get back to the gymnasium before the masters wake up." He pulled on his pants and searched for his shoes in the dim light from the streetlamp outside the bedroom window. "And I am worried about Bohdan." He found his shoes. "Aren't you concerned about Irina?"

She leaned over to kiss him again, and Maurice took the moment to look at her naked breasts one more time in the dim light. He kissed her and left as quietly as he could.

The streets were deserted, silent and dark. Maurice stayed on the minor streets as much as possible, avoiding the broad avenues. He estimated it was about two in the morning when he reached the gymnasium. Scaling the fence was not difficult, and he climbed down a tree just inside the grounds. Climbing to the second-storey dormitory window was only a little more challenging. Students joked that the trees on the grounds had been planted by previous generations just to help them climb out at night.

Maurice eased himself through the open window he and Bohdan had left for themselves earlier, just after bed-check.

I hope he's okay, Maurice thought. *I hope he got home all right.*

He was in the back hallway that led from the dormitory to the stairs. He slipped off his shoes and padded toward the door when light flooded the corridor.

Maurice froze, blinking. At the end of the hallway by the door to the dorm, no longer hidden in shadows, stood Father Ihor, the man responsible for the students and discipline. Bohdan stood beside him, slouched, staring at the floor.

"Good evening, Mr. Bury," Father Ihor said. "I trust you had an entertaining evening."

Does he know about Oksana? How could he? What will he do if he finds out that I...

"Well? What do you have to say?" Father Ihor asked, keeping his voice low so he didn't wake the others.

"I am late because I was...I was hiding..."

"From the police?" Father Ihor's voice rose a little and Maurice could see the anger on his face.

"They weren't real policemen, Father," Bohdan said in a weak voice. He sounded more like a ten-year-old than a senior student.

"Yes, yes, I know that. You've already told me your story, Bohdan. I know the real police did not raid your dance hall. And I appreciate the strife from Polish bullies. But the question is what were you doing in the dance hall in the first place?"

Maurice thought fast. "We were emphasizing and participating in Ukrainian culture."

Father Ihor let himself smile a little at that. "You were

dancing and drinking beer. I can still smell it on Bohdan's breath. Maurice, surely you understand we can't have the pupils sneaking away to cavort and drink and stay out past curfew? And really, in your case, to come home past two in the morning? At least Bohdan was back before midnight, but now you've made him and me stay up for hours longer."

"I'm sorry, Father, but really I was afraid of getting beaten by the Poles—"

"I am far too tired to argue with your lies and nonsense this morning, Maurice. You two will be in my office at eight o'clock promptly, when I will deal with this. Now go to bed, quietly. Do not dare wake your fellow students." Father Ihor strode away and disappeared down the stairs.

Bohdan blew out the breath he had been holding. "I thought we'd get caned for sure. Where the hell were you all this time?" he whispered.

"Oksana pulled me out the side door when the cops came in..."

"They weren't cops, Maurice. Just Polish nationalists in uniforms. They didn't even have police crests on their shoulders."

"I didn't notice that." Maurice felt even more foolish.

"You have to look for things like that. Don't let some idiot in a uniform bully you on the street." He smiled then. "So you've been with Oksana since ten in the evening? You sly dog."

Maurice felt his face heat up, but at that moment the door to the dormitory opened and a sleepy face peered out, squinting in the light. "Will you two shut the hell up? It's two in the morning."

"Sorry," Bohdan and Maurice whispered together. Bohdan shut the hall light and they crept to their beds.

At eight o'clock, Bohdan and Maurice stood outside Father Ihor's office, feeling exactly the same as eight-year-olds outside the principal's office. Father Ihor did not even look at the two students as he came down the main hallway.

Maurice had only taken a step into the priest's office when something banged on the school's front door, followed by the crash of breaking glass. Father Ihor pushed the boys out of his way and ran to the door. "What in Heaven's name..." He was cut off by another smashing window and a rock slid across the floor, along with glittering shards of glass.

Through the broken window in the front door, Maurice saw a group of young men his own age with bats and boards, gathered at the foot of the steps. He could hear them chanting in Polish. "Ukies out. Lwow for Poland." (Lwow was the Polish name for Lviv, the district Peremyshl was part of).

"Get back, Maurice," Father Ihor said. "Go to your class." He started to push the door open when another rock hit the door frame. The priest jumped back, letting the door close.

Bohdan had come to the door too, and pointed out the window to the side of the school. The senior classmen came running around from the back, yelling and carrying bats and sticks and whatever else they could find. The Poles at the steps bunched together, almost in military formation, ready for the attack.

Father Ihor threw the door open and strode out onto the landing at the top of the concrete steps. "Stop it," he said in Polish. "As Catholics, you should all be ashamed." A rock sailed up from the crowd and missed the priest, but he flinched when it crashed through the window. Inside, Maurice and Bohdan jumped back to avoid the flying glass.

The Ukrainian boys yelled again and charged at the Polish crowd. Maurice and Bohdan stepped outside beside Father Ihor and heard a loud whistle. A uniformed man emerged from the crowd at the bottom of the steps, hands held up high. He blew the whistle again and the charging Ukrainian students skidded to a halt.

"What is this, officer? Why are you allowing these ruffians to break my windows?" Father Ihor demanded.

Watching the Ukrainian students, the police officer pulled out his nightstick and blew his whistle again. When he was certain they were standing still, at least for the moment, he turned to the priest at the top of the steps.

"These boys are just a little excited, that's all. A new directive from the Ministry of Education has declared that all Ukrainian schools are to be closed, effective today. They—" He lifted one hand to indicate the Polish men as if he were introducing a choir. "—noticed your Gymnasium is still open."

"That declaration affects the elementary schools, only," Father Ihor shouted back. "The gymnasium has a dispensation from His Holiness the Pope to operate under Polish administration, which was clearly indicated in the promulgation of the law."

Father Ihor started down the steps, angrily shrugging Maurice's hand off his shoulder when he tried to stop him. "Am I to understand you brought these gangsters here? That you are trying to intimidate us? We, who are operating within the scope of the law and under the protection of the Holy See?"

"Nothing of the kind, Father," the officer said, holding up his hands again. "As I said, these boys just got a little carried away. Now that you and I have clarified the situation—" he turned toward the Polish men, who were beginning to murmur among themselves. "They will return home, or to their jobs. Right?"

"What about my broken windows? Who is going to be responsible for replacing them?"

The policeman shrugged. "I'm sorry, Father, I did not see who broke your windows. I cannot hold anyone responsible without eyewitness evidence."

With a smile, the policeman turned toward the crowd of Polish men at the bottom of the stairs. "All right, men, that's enough for now. You heard the Father. The gymnasium has dispensation from His Holiness. Go on, now, you all have better things to do."

Slowly, with glances toward the Ukrainian crowd to the side, the men lowered their bats and clubs and walked away in pairs and small groups. Father Ihor, Bohdan and Maurice watched them go. When the sidewalk was clear, Father Ihor spoke to the upperclassmen. "I appreciate your willingness to defend your gymnasium, but I think it's best you don't try to fight with a mob again. It will only lead to tragedy."

"What are we supposed to do, Father," said someone in the crowd. "Turn the other cheek?"

Father Ihor nodded. "As our Lord commands. Now go on, you also have better things to do. Back to classes."

As the seniors disappeared around the back of the school again, Father Ihor turned to Maurice and Bohdan on the steps with him. "Don't think I've forgotten about your tricks last night. I forgive you, but given what's happening these days, I think it's best you don't go off the school grounds unless at least four of you are together. Understand? Now, go to your classes."

Chapter 14: Escape

Kharkiv, November, 1941

Maurice woke when the house was still dark. Joachim's maid stood beside the sofa, a bundle of cloth in her arms. "Clean clothes for you to wear," she said, and left the room.

The pants were too wide and too short, the shirt loose and the sleeves short, but they were clean and soft.

He padded to the kitchen, where the maid had set bread and tea on the table. She did not even look at him and Maurice saw her hands shaking as she puttered around, putting things away or wiping counters. He ate without saying anything and swallowed the hot tea as quickly as he could.

Joachim came into the kitchen, wearing another expensive suit. He nodded at the maid and she left.

Joachim sat across from Maurice. "You slept well?"

"Thank you. You've been very kind."

Joachim held his eye. "Kindness had nothing to do with it. We three—you, me, Lieutenant Daniel—all need each other."

"What does Bohdan—Daniel need?"

"Now that Hauptman Daniel has helped you, he needs you to succeed in getting back home or he'll be shot. He may be shot even if you do succeed, you know."

At the sound of loud knocking, Joachim sighed and stood. Despite his fine clothes, he looked worn and weary. Maurice followed him to the front door, where the little maid hesitated before opening it.

"Stop. I had better get it," Joachim said. "You should stay out of the sight of soldiers as much as possible, my dear."

Joachim opened the door to see Daniel with a strangely familiar German soldier—not the one who had brought him the day before. Maurice first saw the soldier had no weapon before he realized it was his sergeant, Petro, in a German uniform. He held a bundle of clothing like the maid had a half-hour earlier. Beyond the broken wall on the road, an open-back truck waited with the rest of Maurice's odalenye, all in civilian clothes, and three armed German soldiers. Maurice looked at them carefully. They weren't the same soldiers as yesterday.

"Get changed," Daniel said as Petro held the clothes out. Maurice took them and Daniel stepped inside the house, closing the door on the others.

Maurice stripped quickly in the hallway. Only when he was in his underwear did he wonder, briefly, about women in the house. Where had the little maid gone? And Joachim's family—he had mentioned them the day before, but Maurice hadn't seen them. He must have ordered them to stay out of the sight of soldiers, like the maid.

The clothes were another German officer's uniform. "It's my spare," Daniel said. It was about the right size, if loose because of all the weight Maurice had lost. He carefully fastened every button. Daniel tugged the shoulders and sleeves and smoothed the shoulders until he looked almost acceptable as a German officer—*one that had been drinking for days without eating,* Maurice thought, as he looked in Joachim's hallway mirror.

"Fold up those clothes," Daniel told Petro. "Take them with you." He took an envelope from inside his jacket and pulled out a sheaf of papers, each bearing an official

Luftwaffe stamp. Maurice was not used to reading Roman letters anymore, and it took him some time to understand the words. Mixed among them were five ten-ruble notes.

"Passes across Ukraine," Daniel said as he led Maurice to the truck. You're all skilled machinists, authorized to use trains and to borrow rides on trucks or whatever to get back to Ternopyl. You also have a border pass you'll need when you get to Halychyna—that's part of the *generalgouvernement* now, a German colony in Ukraine. It's not part of the *Reichskommissariat*, occupied Ukraine."

"Why?" Maurice could not believe this was happening. He had asked, but he had never believed his old friend would be able to make this happen.

Daniel did not answer, but led Maurice outside to the truck. He ordered the prisoners, Maurice's odalenye, to climb down. "You men are here to repair this wall." He turned to the driver. "You can return to the camp now. The three of us—" He indicated Maurice and Petro in German uniforms, although without weapons. "—are enough to guard this group of Slavs while they repair these quarters for the general's son."

"What's so special about him?" the driver asked, pointing to Maurice.

Can he tell the uniform doesn't fit me properly? Maurice wondered.

"Are you questioning an officer's orders?" Daniel said. "The colonel has work for you to do back at the camp, so don't make him wait. Go."

The driver glared at Maurice again, but put the truck into gear and drove away, shaking his head.

"All right, boys, you heard me. Get to work. Clear up the debris, stack it by the road. Has anyone here done masonry?"

"I did a little at home," Big Eugene said.

"Good. See if you can sort out some bricks or stones to repair this wall. Maurice, you get some clothes from Joachim for your men. You won't make it across the country in Red Army uniforms."

The men started picking up broken bricks and stones. Eugene made a stack of his own, while Petro tried to give the impression of guarding the team, watching for any escape attempt.

Joachim looked shocked when Maurice asked him for clothes. "Ten suits you want? What am I supposed to wear?"

"You need us gone from your house as fast as possible, and we need clothes. I don't care if they're old or dirty. They can't be worse than what they're wearing now."

"My clothes won't fit all of your men, especially that giant lout over there." He pointed at Eugene.

Maurice was losing patience with his reluctant host. He did not know Daniel's plan, but he felt he was running out of time. "We'll make do. Hurry."

It was nearly an hour before Joachim returned with a stack of clothes. His maid followed with more. "Here. Ten pants, ten shirts. I have a couple of jackets too, and three old hats. No shoes, though."

"We'll make do." Maurice opened the door a crack, where the men were still pretending to work on Joachim's garden wall. *A useless pretence,* Maurice thought. There was no traffic on the streets, not a German in sight. Maurice called Orest and Viktor to him. "Pick out a pair of pants and a shirt and change into them. Mr. Joachim, please burn their uniforms."

Maurice sorted through the pile, looking for the largest set for Eugene. Orest and Viktor changed and put their old, worn boots back on and returned to work. Two by two, the men came in and changed clothes. Wrinkling their noses, Joachim and his maid picked up the discarded Soviet uniforms and took them to the furnace.

With the odalenye in civilian clothing, except for Maurice and Petro in their German uniforms, Daniel gathered them at Joachim's broken gate.

"Next step: we are walking in good order to the train

station. All together, but not military style. No marching. You are civilians, machinists who will work in German factories in western Ukraine. Poland. Stay together, stay quiet. No chattering. Walk quickly but not too fast, and follow me. Maurice and Petro, you will bring up the rear. Understand?"

The men nodded. Maurice could see they were all nervous: they looked quickly over their shoulers, and hunched forward as if to make themselves smaller. Maurice was also afraid the whole thing was a trick. He thought the truck would come back at any moment, carrying a full company of German guards. Or to hear a machine gun and see his men fall.

We were as good as dead of starvation or disease in the camp, though.

He ran back to Joachim's front door, where the man stood, watching them. Maurice shook his hand. "Thank you," he said, and couldn't think of anything else to say. "Thank you."

Joachim said nothing, but nodded.

The odalenye followed Daniel through Kharkiv's broken streets. There was almost no traffic, but the Germans had set up checkpoints every few blocks, and the guards looked suspiciously at thirteen walking men. Each time, Daniel showed them a pass he carried. "These skilled machinists are being transported east to the factories," Daniel said, over and over again.

One junior officer kept his sidearm in his hand as he examined Daniel's pass. Maurice could not take his eyes from it, nor could he stop shaking. Daniel noticed. "Damn it, Moritz, if you can't pull yourself together in the morning, you shouldn't stay up all night drinking," he said. His name in German sounded so strange to Maurice. "You know, if you weren't the general's son, you'd be court-martialed." Daniel gave the junior officer a look that seemed to say, "What can you do?" The officer returned the paper to Daniel, but as the group passed, Maurice saw him pick up a telephone handset.

After a two-hour walk, they arrived at a minor train station on the outskirts of the city. The few soldiers guarding it were not German.

"Romanian auxiliaries. They're shit in battle, but they make adequate guards for a train station," Daniel said.

On the platform, Maurice felt surreal, seeing his sergeant in a German uniform and the ten of his men in civilian clothes, almost as if there were on their way to college.

Daniel brought him back to earth. "Do you have the papers?"

Maurice held them out. "Keep them safe, Lieutenant Bauer," Daniel said, looking very much a German officer at that point: back straight, chin high, every bit of his uniform in its proper place.

Maurice folded the papers carefully but quickly and shoved them into his jacket. "You will follow that plan to the letter, do you understand? Deviate one metre from it and you will be shot."

"Why have you done this?" Maurice asked. "Why take such a risk?"

Bohdan's face showed no expression. "You are my friend, Maurice. My best friend from the gymnasium in Peremyshl." He leaned closer and his voice went lower again as he switched into Ukrainian. "We had such hopes in 1940. That was why I joined the army. Then Hitler arrested the Ukrainian government and sent them all to a concentration camp."

Maurice nodded. "I know."

Bohdan straightened and, still expressionless, said "Tell your sister hello from Bohdan."

He did this for my sister? Maurice wondered. *He only met her once! No,* he realized. *He did it for me.*

Daniel turned smartly on his heel, like a proper German officer, and strode to the gate. A tear slid down Maurice's face as Bohdan disappeared from view.

He never saw him again.

Then all his men were around him, clamouring, slapping him on the back. "How did you do it? Thank you. I can't believe it, Lieutenant—"

"Stop it," Maurice said. "Stand back, men. I am not your friend. I am Leutnant Moritz Bauer, and I am responsible for transporting you...civilians back east to work in German factories. From now on, no familiarity. You will address me as 'Herr Leutnant,' and you will speak in low voices. I am holding the papers that will get us past checkpoints to Ternopyl—no, Petro, not to Lviv, sorry, you'll have to work that part out on your own."

He led them into the station canteen, where they crowded around two tables. Maurice spent one of the ten-ruble notes on soup for all of them. "Kyiv borshcht," beet soup with potatoes and eggs in it.

A freight train pulled along the platform, bells ringing. An official walked down the platform calling, "Points west: Poltava, Lubny, Kyiv." The boys gulped as much soup as they could and scrambled out, Maurice bringing up the rear.

Do I look like a German officer? he wondered. *Will they believe me?*

He felt his heart pounding as a train inspector approached. "I am escorting these men west, to Ternopyl," Maurice said in German. He showed the inspector the papers Bohdan had given him. He struggled not to tremble.

The inspector looked at the papers with the Luftwaffe eagle-stamp. Maurice could see he could not read the Roman lettering. "There is no more room on the passenger cars," he said in broken German. "You'll have to ride in an empty freight car."

"All right," Maurice said. *Would a real German officer do that?*

The inspector pointed at an empty car and left them alone without another word.

Maurice and his men climbed into the empty car and tried to find a relatively safe place to sit. They pulled the door most of the way closed, leaving it just open enough to watch Kharkiv and their imprisonment slip behind them.

"What did you eat yesterday?" Maurice asked Petro, his sergeant. *My former sergeant,* he thought.

"A bit of crust of bread each and water." His face was drawn with dark circles under his eyes and deep lines down his cheeks.

There is no way he could pass for a real German sergeant, Maurice thought. *The Germans are not underfed. Underfed. Deliberately starved. We have escaped. But to what? An occupied country. And will the Germans let us resettle, or arrest us again?*

Chapter 15: On the train

Across Ukraine, November, 1941

"Why do you look so unhappy?"

Maurice did not know what to say to the woman in from of him on the train platform. He barely had the strength to say anything.

He knew he and his dozen men looked out of place. Everyone else there was either female, old or a child. It seemed the war had taken every young man. And there they were, twelve men of service age, all looking hungry and desperate.

"Why are you so unhappy?" she said again. "You must be hungry." She stepped closer, into the light that spilled thorough the station window, shielded from above in an effort to thwart German bombers. He saw she was older than he thought at first, in her forties, but tired and worn many years beyond that. She was thin and grey with deep lines down her face. Her clothes were threadbare, even the kerchief over her hair. He wondered if he looked as weary as she did.

"I am," he said.

"My son is your age. I don't know whether he is alive or dead." She took some banknotes out of her purse.

"Here is five rubles. Go get some porridge in the canteen."

Maurice hesitated and the woman pushed the money into his hand. Over her head, a sign swung in the wind, squeaking. Wynyca. Maurice had never heard of the town or village or whatever it was. *How far are we from Kharkiv?* he wondered. *How much farther to go to Ternopyl?*

"Dyakuyu," he said, and turned to his men. He led his boys into the canteen. Five rubles would buy enough porridge for all twelve of them. Compared to what they had got at the POW camp, it was a feast.

The boys sat at little white-painted tables or stood, gobbling porridge as fast as they could. No one spilled a drop. Soon their spirits lifted, their voices rose and a couple even laughed. Maurice did not know how to thank the woman enough, but when he looked at the platform, she was gone.

It had been only one day since Bohdan had shown up at Joachim's house and handed Maurice their passes to ride trains. One day of finding how to keep the train's motion from throwing them across an empty box-car.

Maurice had changed back into the clothes Joachim had given him and thrown the spare German uniform by the tracks when he could no longer see Kharkiv behind them. He wondered again how much longer it would take to cross Ukraine. How many checkpoints would there be? How many times would Bohdan's—no, Daniel's—passes satisfy the Germans?

The train's whistle blew. It had restocked with coal and water and was ready to leave again. Maurice and his boys scooped up the rest of their porridge and jumped into their empty freight car as it began to move. Maurice took one more look for the woman who had given him money. He had not even asked her name. He sat on the floor, back against the side of the boxcar and watched the dark country slip by until, against his will, he fell asleep.

Maurice started. Outside the half-open door it was dark. He could barely make out Petro beside him. "How long was I sleeping?"

Petro laughed. "All night and all the next day. We didn't have the heart to wake you. Did you know you snore louder than the train?" He handed Maurice an apple. "A couple of the boys managed to scrounge up a barrel of apples and some water. Go ahead. You must be hungry."

Maurice took a big bite of the most delicious apple he had ever tasted. He staggered to the door, braced one shoulder against it and relieved himself out the opening, careful not to fall outside as the train rocked. Then he took a metal bottle of tepid water from Nikolai before lying on the hard floor and drifting into sleep again.

Sunrise woke him as the train pulled into another small town. Maurice saw pairs of inspectors in Romanian uniforms walking down the length of the train, peering into each car. Two pairs entered the passenger cars at the front of the train.

Another pair worked their way down the freight cars. When the sergeant looked into the car with Maurice and his men, he jumped back a step, eyes wide. "Who are you and what are you doing in here?" he asked in German. The private stepped forward, rifle pointing vaguely into the boxcar.

Maurice held out their passes. The sergeant took a cautious step closer to the train and peered at the paper, frowning. Maurice wondered if he could read or understand the language, but the official stamp seemed to satisfy him. He looked up. "Where are you going?"

"We're machinists, heading to Ternopyl. The Germans want us to work in a factory there," he said, hoping he sounded like a working man and not like a soldier. *How do soldiers sound?* he wondered.

"Why are you in a freight car?"

Maurice shrugged. "There were no places on the passenger cars." That, at least, was true.

The sergeant frowned again. Maurice thought he did not believe him. Then he heard shouts from further down the train. Maurice, the sergeant and the soldier all turned to look, and the boys on the car leaned out to see, too.

Romanian guards were pulling two men in ragged clothing from the last car. More guards ran toward them, weapons aimed. Two climbed into the boxcar and three more stowaways tumbled out.

The guards pushed the men onto their knees and a sergeant demanded their papers again. Maurice saw one of the prisoners tremble, another shake his head.

The soldier who had come to the car with Maurice and his men looked at his sergeant, waiting for an order. But the sergeant seemed frozen in place, staring at the tableau at the end of the train. One hand still held Maurice's passes.

"Spies," said the sergeant at the end of the train. One of the stowaways raised his hands as if he were praying. Then came a rapid volley of shots. *Pop-pop-pop-pop-pop.* The stowaways fell without making a sound.

Maurice realized his mouth was open, and so was the sergeant's. Behind him, he heard one of his men groan.

The sergeant turned to Maurice, glanced at the papers again and shoved them back at Maurice. He hesitated as if to say something, but decided against it. He turned away and walked back to the station. The soldier slung his rifle over his shoulder and trotted after him.

Maurice and his men looked back at the train. A Romanian soldier drove a horse-drawn wagon to the site and the soldiers threw the bodies onto it.

The whistle sounded, the engine groaned and the wheels squealed. Slowly, the train moved out of the station. Maurice turned to look at his men. No one said anything.

In the late afternoon, the train stopped at a station in an old city, Volochysk. Ahead, they could see a river, but across the tracks were heavy gates. German soldiers guarded it, standing in towers on both sides of the tracks.

"The Zbruch River," Private Ivan said. "We're only

fifty kilometres from home."

"We have to get past the German guards, first," Petro said.

The Zbruch was once the border between the Ukrainian Soviet Socialist Republic and pre-war Poland. Now, it separated the Generalgouvernement and Reichskommissariat Ukraine, or military-occupied Ukraine. Daniel told him this would be the most difficult crossing, where the scrutiny of the passes would be the most exacting.

"I can't wait to see my Katerinya," Andrei said.

"I can't wait to eat my mother's soup," Orest said.

The brakes squealed and they lurched forward. The train stopped in a wide yard. Ranks of tracks paralleled their own.

The half-open door was wrenched wide and two Wehrmacht guards poked sub-machine guns inside. If they were shocked to see twelve men inside, their faces did not show it.

Maurice felt his heart hammering in his chest. *Will Daniel's papers satisfy them?*

A sergeant climbed in. "Papers," he said. He looked like he expected them not to have documents, and his eyes widened in surprise when Andreij, the youngest of Maurice's boys, handed him a wrinkled, dog-eared slip. The sergeant snatched it from Andreij, looked at it carefully, snorted and gave it back, then snatched the document from the next man, and then from Maurice. Maurice watched the sergeant read the travel authorization, the officer's signature, and the stamp, "Kharkov."

The sergeant's eyebrows rose at that point. "You're from the front lines?" he said.

Maurice just nodded. *Don't say anything you don't have to.*

The sergeant gave Maurice his paper then went on to check the rest of the men in the car. Disappointed not to find anyone travelling improperly, he ordered his men to the next car and jumped out. Soldiers pulled the door shut again. As it slid into place, Maurice could see soldiers all down the length the train pulling hapless men out, marching them with their hands in the air into the night.

When had they climbed aboard? he wondered. But he had no emotion left to worry about them.

The whistle blew, the train lurched forward and Petro fell on his butt.

Silently, they watched the river pass beneath them. They exhaled as one.

The November evening was deep black when the train pulled into the Ternopyl station. The boys jumped off and showed more German guards their papers.

"Goodbye, Meroslaw," Petro said. "And thank you. God, I don't know what to say. I don't know how you got us out of that camp, let alone across the country." They embraced.

The other boys gathered around. Andrei kissed him on both cheeks, then kissed all the others, and soon they were all saying goodbye, pounding each other on the back, hugging. "Keep it down, boys," someone said. They were all conscious of the frowns from the guards.

They were torn between the desire to go home and the bond formed in war and prison. Home won. Maurice knew it was better if they split up. At every train station and check-point, he had seen the guards' suspicion at twelve non-uniformed men traveling together in wartime.

Thank you again, Bohdan, he thought.

He was alone in the city. Nastaciv, the village where his mother lived, was nearly twenty kilometres away—two hours on horseback or wagon, half a day's journey on foot, and he was exhausted. And the German curfew would fall soon.

He could turn to only one person in the city. Maurice started for the house of his old teacher and then supervisor from the Ridna Shkola, Professor Posmychuck. It took him two hours to find his house in the dark.

Maurice knocked on the back-door window. No answer. He knocked again, harder. Somewhere inside, he heard someone moving. Still, no one came to the window or door. Maurice understood. After dark, in wartime, in an occupation by a hostile force, he would not have answered a knock at the window, either.

"Open up," he said, torn between the desire to be heard inside and not to be heard by anyone outside. "It's me, Maurice."

He heard soft footfalls and then, slowly and carefully, the back door opened a crack.

"Who is it?"

"It's me, Maurice Bury," he said again. "I'm back."

The door opened a little more, and he saw the bearded face of Professor Posmychuck, a small man in a tattered dressing gown. In the shadows behind him, Maurice could see Mrs. Posmychuck. She was shaking.

"Maurice?" The professor peered at him in the gloom and flicked on a light in the kitchen. Maurice stepped into the light. "You look familiar, but you don't look like the Maurice Bury I knew."

"I know. I don't recognize myself. But it's me."

"I heard Maurice Bury was dead, killed on the front lines."

"No, no, it's me. My mother is Tekla Kuritsa, my sister is Hanya. We all live in Nastasciu, eighteen kilometres away in the country. I know your brother, Stefan, he was studying medicine…"

The door swung open and Mrs. Posmychuck swept her arms around him. "Maurice, oh Maurice," she said over and over. "Oh, your mother will be so happy." She let him go and Maurice could see tears on her face.

They shut the door quickly and Mrs. Posmychuck told him to sit at the kitchen table as she made tea. She cut him a thick piece of bread. Her hands shook as she put honey on it. Maurice had to tell the professor everything about his journey across Ukraine while he ate. He did not mention Bohdan or the POW camp. He focused on the trains, about how the Germans searched them at the Zbruch crossing, how his papers got him through the checkpoint. The professor kept nodding, but did not actually say anything.

"Eat up, Maurice," Mrs. Posmychuck said repeatedly. "Would you like some more bread?"

The Professor poured each of them a measure of vodka when Maurice finished his story. "Well, Maurice, I think you have much more to tell me, or maybe it's best I don't know. But you must be very tired. Do you even know what time it is? Come upstairs, we have a spare bed for…"

"Oh, no, professor, I can't sleep in your bed," Maurice said.

"No, not in my bed, an extra bed. One we have for overnight guests."

"No, I can't sleep in any bed in your house."

"Why not?"

"Because I'm full of lice."

The professor and his wife looked shocked. "I see. Well, thank you for telling us." They were uncomfortable, unsure of what to do.

"Why don't I sleep on the chair? It will be much better than I've become used to."

Mrs. Posmychuck brought him two old blankets, and she and her husband went upstairs again for the night, leaving Maurice to a restless doze.

In the morning, the Posmychucks gave Maurice the biggest breakfast they could muster in the wartime shortages: thick slices of home-made bread, eggs and tea. The professor kept asking Maurice questions. "Did you ever see anyone else from the gymnasium? Anyone else you knew from Lviv or Ternopyl?"

"Strangely enough, no one I knew." *Except for Bohdan, but I had better not mention him,* Maurice thought.

"Did you do much fighting?"

"Mostly retreating. But I think it's better if I do not tell you much. Better for both of us," Maurice said. "In fact, professor, while I am very grateful for your help, I need for you not to mention me to anyone."

The professor nodded and looked at his tea for a minute. "I understand, Maurice. Oh, this war—it has forced a terrible simplification on our nation."

"What do you mean?"

"Many Ukrainians were happy when the Germans invaded. They pushed the communists out. Did you know some village women even brought the soldiers flowers?"

"We heard stories like that," Maurice said.

"I myself, I was happy, too. No more communists. I thought we were free. Free of the Russians and the Poles, too. We all thought so. Melnyk declared a free Ukrainian government at the end of June. For a moment, a flicker of hope..." Posmychuk's lips compressed into a line and Maurice could see the anger in his eyes.

"In a week, the Germans arrested the whole cabinet. No one has heard of them since, but to me, it's obvious. They were shot, every one of them. We're no more free now than we ever were under Stalin. Even the Poles were better than this. We're not a country. We're part of what the Germans call the Generalgouvernment, a colony of Germany. We Ukrainians, and the Poles and the Russians too, we have to make room for the Germans. For their liebensraum."

"Make room? How?"

The professor leaned closer and spoke in a hoarse whisper. "We'll have to clear out. First the Jews. Then anyone Slavic—Poles, Ukrainians, Russians, whatever. Hitler wants Ukrainian land for Germans. I heard there is a plan to breed Ukrainian girls with German soldiers, to create a strong worker race. A whole sub-species just to work on German farms, serve German people."

"So the Germans plan on staying here."

The professor nodded. "This is a conquest. When the Germans win this war, they're going to get rid of the Ukrainians and the Jews." He gulped the remainder of his tea and stood. "Well, I had better go now, or I'll be late."

"Is the Ridna Shkola open?"

"Oh, yes. The Germans value education. But—" He sighed as he fastened his briefcase. "They are strict about the content."

Mrs. Posmychuk came into the kitchen with a bundle of clothing. "Here are some of the professor's old things," she said. "Now, don't argue, Maurice. You can't put those clothes on again—they're positively infested with lice."

"Where are my clothes?" Maurice asked.

"In the furnace," she said, smiling.

The professor kissed Maurice on both cheeks and left for the college. Maurice went into a bedroom to change into the professor's old clothes. They did not fit very well, but they were clean.

He helped Mrs. Posmychuk clean the kitchen, thanked her a hundred times, kissed her at the door. She would not let him leave without eating another thick slice of bread and taking half a loaf with him. Maurice's empty stomach would not let him leave without it, either.

Finally, he stepped into a cold, clear November morning in Ternopyl. *Now, all I need is some way back to the farm.* He walked to the farmers' market.

Even though it was wartime, the market bustled as farmers sold the last of their harvests: corn, wheat, parsley, apples, pears, onions and beets. Townspeople pressed through the stalls, haggling over vegetables, chickens and animal feed. Behind a stall selling eggs stood a slim woman whose dark brown hair threatened to burst the knot in her kerchief.

Maurice tapped her on the shoulder. "Hello, Tekla."

The woman spun to face him, expecting trouble. She glared at him for several seconds before her eyes widened.

"Maurice? My god, I cannot believe it." She wrapped her arms around him and squeezed tight. She had to lean over her table of eggs, but she held on. Maurice hugged back, wary of knocking eggs down. When she let him go, she looked at him as if she were afraid he was about to vanish again. "What are you doing here?"

Tekla was his cousin, daughter of Myhailo Kuritsa, his mother's brother. She had been named after her aunt.

"I'm coming home. Can you give me a ride?" he asked.

She threw her arms around him again. "Of course, Maurice, of course. Oh, I can't believe it. We heard you'd been…been killed." She held him at arm's length. "You're so thin. You must have been starving." She called to the woman in the stand next to hers, who had been staring at them. "Hanyah, please, sell the eggs for me."

"Of course, dear. Take the young man home and give him something to eat. Right away," Hanyah said. She was older than Maurice's mother, and Maurice did not know her, but she smiled at him as if he were a grandchild she had not seen for a year.

Tekla re-tied her scarf and pulled on her gloves, took Maurice by the hand and led him out of the market. "My wagon is over here," she said, then stopped. "You know what we should do, Maurice? Let's get a picture together."

"Can't we..."

But Tekla interrupted, took his hand and led him through the market to a small shop, were she paid a few rubles for a picture. The photographer had Maurice sit on a stool in front of a cloth draped against the wall, and posed Tekla standing next to him. Tekla could not stop smiling, nor babbling.

"I can't wait to see Auntie's face when she sees you standing on her doorstep. Oh, and my father, too. It's too bad your father is not here, Maurice. He would be so relieved, so happy to know you're home safe. Are you sure this is my better side?" She asked the photographer as he adjusted the camera. He smiled, nodded and calmly pressed the shutter.

"The print will be ready on Thursday," the photographer said and handed Tekla a ticket. "Welcome back, friend," he said to Maurice.

As they climbed into Tekla's wagon, she said, "We'll go to my mother's house first. It's closer, and we'll send someone to tell your mother you've come home." She elaborated her plans as she drove out of the city. On the way, the roads became rougher and finally became just dirt tracks.

Maurice thought about her words, when she said everyone had feared he'd been killed. *Professor Posmychuk had said the same thing. Did it mean someone had seen Hrech Kowalchuk's dead body—is my double now dead? Is that what poor Hrech had meant when he said, "It's going to be important one day for people to mistake us for one another?"*

Mikhailo Kuritsa's farmhouse was modern for the area, two stories of whitewashed stone. In midmorning, it was empty. Mikhailo was working either in the fields or among the outbuildings. Maurice wondered whether his son, Tekla's brother, had been drafted by the Reds too, whether he was alive or dead. But he could not bring himself to ask and risk spoiling Tekla's mood.

"Sit on the *skrena*," Tekla said, pointing a large wooden chest for linens that marked the division between the kitchen and the sitting room. "Mama's in the garden." She skipped out the back door.

Cool fall air blew in through the open door. Maurice heard Tekla and her mother. "I've brought home a released prisoner who wants to know if he can sleep here," Tekla said.

"What," her mother cried. "No, no, it's too dangerous. What if the police come?"

"But Mama, he needs our help. Besides, I think you'll like him."

"Like him? What's the matter with you?"

"Just come in and see him, Mama."

"I have no patience for your games, Tekla."

Tekla shook her head in good-natured exasperation as she pulled her mother by the arm into the house. Evdokia continued to argue. "I will give him something to eat, but he cannot—what are you laughing about?"

"Hello, Aunt Evdokia," Maurice said.

The older woman stepped back in shock, eyes wide. One hand touched her throat, and the other clutched her daughter's hand.

"It's not true," she said, sputtering after nearly a minute filled with the musical sound of Tekla's laughter. "You were killed, Maurice." He stood, but Evdokia ran out of the house, calling her husband and all the neighbours. "Come on. Quickly. Maurice Bury has returned home."

In minutes, the little farmhouse was filled with people hugging, kissing and shaking hands with Maurice. Food appeared on the table. Someone brought out the vodka and men began to sing. Neighbours embraced him, kissed his cheeks, demanded stories. Young boys kept asking about the Germans.

"How big are the tanks?"

"Ours are bigger, but the Panzers are faster," he would say.

"Did you see any airplanes?"

"Yes, many. Mostly German."

"Did you kill any Germans?"

"I'm not sure."

"Were you hurt?"

He told them about being hit by shrapnel outside Kyiv. Singing and conversations stopped as the neighbours drew closer to see Maurice lift his pant leg and show the scars on his calf and knee. "We were getting off the train, when two of the Messerschmidt fighters began strafing us. Everyone dropped and scattered. A lot of boys got killed."

"How did you get hurt, though?" asked Mihail Babiak, a man just a few years older than Maurice who lived a few kilometres away. Maurice wondered how he had avoided induction by the Reds.

"Shrapnel," he said. "Bullets hit the wooden ramp and huge splinters went into my leg. The surgeons wanted to cut it off, but I found one good, old doctor who saved it."

"My God," Mihail said, shaking his head. He gulped down more vodka before collapsing onto an empty chair.

Maurice avoided talking about his capture and his release by Bohdan. "The fighting is past us now, probably completely past Ukraine," he said. "The Germans are fighting in Russia."

"Let the Russians fight," one man said, but Maurice could not see who it was.

It had been a long, long time since Maurice's belly had felt full. For a little while, the warmth, the community and the love pushed away the horrors of the battlefield, the march, the prison camp and the trek home. He laughed, kissed his relatives and the pretty girls from the village.

Hrech Zazulak came and stood beside Maurice. "It's good to have one of our boys come back. We have lost so many."

Zazulak was a tall, thin man with thinning dark hair and thick eyebrows, who worked in a machine shop. Maurice was surprised to see him there. He knew him only slightly, and as far as he knew, had never been a close friend of his mother's.

"Thank you," was all he could think to say.

"So, you were in the Red Army for what, six months?"

"Yes, more or less."

"Fought the Germans, eh?"

"Yes. What do you want, Zazulak?"

Zazulak leaned close and spoke low so no one else could hear. "The fighting is not over yet, my friend. Some people continue to fight the conqueror even today."

Maurice stepped back. "Well, my fighting is over."

"You're going to give up so easily?"

"Easily? I nearly lost a leg. What fighting did you do?"

Zazulak straightened and patted Maurice on the shoulder. "When you're ready, why don't you come and see me."

"I don't think so, Zazulak. Aunt Evdokia, please, I'd like to see my mother." He wondered why she had not arrived at her brother's place yet. Tekla had promised to send someone.

Tekla took him back to her wagon and they set out toward his mother's farm. Twenty minutes later, Maurice felt dismay when they arrived. His mother's house was dark and empty. "I don't understand—where have they gone?"

Maurice was quiet and nervous on the ride back to his aunt's, until he saw a familiar wagon and horse in front. He jumped down just in time to see his mother and sister step out of the house. "Mama."

Maurice wrapped his arms around her. Her face pressed into the familiar spot on his chest, just like it had before he left for the army. As he had for years, Maurice pushed his nose down into her hair, inhaling her familiar scent of soap and fresh herbs. For a second, he was a boy again as his mother squeezed his back and sobbed. His sister Hanya wrapped her arms around his shoulders and wet his face with tears as she kissed him.

Only when Maurice's whole body shuddered as he breathed in did he realize he was crying, too. He held his mother and sister as tight as he could until excited neighbours pulled them apart and pressed yet more cups of vodka into their hands.

Once more, Maurice had to recount his journey, tell stories about fighting. He drank toast after toast, stuffed himself with cakes and fruit. Finally he had to go home.

In his old bedroom, Maurice carefully placed an old sheet over his bed. He washed as thoroughly as he could and combed as many lice out of his hair as possible. He pulled on a familiar set of pajamas and tossed his lice-ridden clothes out the window. He would move them into the trash heap the next day.

In the morning, Maurice saw a thin stranger in his mirror, a gaunt, haggard old man. Dark shadows creased his sunken cheeks. Black half-moons hung under his red-rimmed eyes. He could count his ribs. His arms and elbows were red and bruised. His fingernails were black and his hands were stained. No wonder his mother had cried.

Chapter 16: Fighting in their own way

Nastaciv, December 1941

Out of uniform, out of the army, out of prison, Maurice was now under the command of his mother. Tekla Kuritsa did not allow her son to do anything but rest for a whole month. The harvest over, she paid young local boys to do what remained: manuring fields and fixing fences.

Day by day, Maurice regained weight and strength. At first, he sat in the kitchen, drinking tea and reading newspapers.

Nothing but German-approved propaganda. This paper actually says we Ukrainians are happy to be occupied by Germany.

Idleness quickly lost its allure. Maurice decided to make sure the farm was ready for winter. He started with chopping firewood. Just a half-hour a day, relishing in his ability to split logs with a single blow, chopping and sawing harder, and lasting longer each day.

One evening, Tekla took Maurice to the shed beside the barn for a chore he would find much more enjoyable.

"Is that a still?" he asked. "Mama, are you making vodka?"

"It's not very good, but the German officers like it," she said. She set him to work.

Maurice liked the opportunity to concentrate on a task,

drawing a spoonful of clear liquor, carefully closing the valve then setting fire to the spoon. If the liquor burned with a blue flame, it was "proof," good enough for sale.

One evening, Maurice filled six four-litre jugs and put them on a small wagon.

"Good boy," Tekla said and buttoned her coat. "I'll take this to the village."

"Why?"

"To sell to anyone who wants it, of course. But mostly it goes to German officers."

"It's getting too late to go out, Mama," Maurice said. "It's almost curfew."

"That's the time men want to buy vodka," she said, buttoning her coat.

"It's too dangerous for a woman out in the evening. Let me go."

She shook her head. "Maurice, you strong men don't know how things work in wartime," she said, patting his cheek. "An old lady out in the evening is much safer than a man. What would the patrols do if they caught you out after curfew?"

"Throw me in jail."

"They would probably shoot you on the spot, sweetie. But they see an old lady struggling with a heavy wagon, they think of their own mothers."

"Some of these bastards would just as soon shoot their own mothers."

"That's when I sell them some vodka." She smiled and kissed him.

Maurice watched her pull the wagon to the road until she vanished into the evening gloom. He did not realize he was smiling as he shook his head.

My mother. After all I've been through, she's going to sell cheap liquor to the Germans. She's the bravest person I've ever seen.

The End

Preview of Book 2: Tekla and the spy

Nastaciv, Ukraine, January 1942

Knocking, insistent yet soft and rapid, woke Maurice. A little greyness leaked around the blind over his window.

Knocking on the door before dawn during wartime could not be good.

Maurice padded silently to his door and peeked down the hall. His heart was beating fast and sweat beaded his forehead, even though the floorboards sent chills all the way up his legs.

His mother, Tekla, stood at the front door, holding her housecoat closed at her throat with one hand while opening the lock with the other. She opened the door just enough to look outside. "What do you want?" she said, and only her children would know from her tone that she was more scared than angry.

"Tesla? Tesla Kuritsa?"

The similarity between Tesla and Tekla, his mother, had caused a lot of confusion over the years. Tesla lived across the river, married to Maurice's mother's cousin.

"Who are you?" Maurice's mother said.

"Andrieski."

"I don't know any Andrieski."

A long silence followed.

Maurice crept closer, calculating the moves necessary to get the shotgun from its case if the man at the door tried to force his way in. *Would I be able to get a clear shot without hitting my mother? Mama, get away from the door.*

"What did you say?" Tekla said to the man at the door.

Maurice crept a little closer and heard the man whisper, but he could not make out any words.

"No one is allowed outdoors at this time of the morning," Tekla said. "You had better clear out before you get us both in trouble."

"Are you not Tesla Kuritsa?" the man said. Maurice could hear desperation in his voice.

"No, I am not. Now clear off."

"It's all right. You can admit it. I am...a comrade."

Maurice's breath caught in his throat. *A communist—a Soviet agent. He's trying to make contact with Tesla Kuritsa.*

"You're no comrade of mine, mister. I am not Tesla Kuritsa. Now get out before I shoot you myself." She pushed the door closed and locked it before turning around and leaning on it. Even in the dark, Maurice could see her shaking.

Maurice shook his head to tell her not to speak, then stepped to the front window. He used one finger to move the curtains just enough to see a man walk to the road. He wore warm winter clothing and carried a bag over his shoulder. He looked like any of hundreds of working men, but Maurice knew who he worked for: Moscow.

Maurice watched the man until he disappeared down the road, then quickly dressed. He let his mother give him a breakfast of kasha and tea and was out the door by the time the sun turned the sky yellow.

On the doorstep, he turned and embraced his mother. He could feel her shaking in his arms. He realized this was only the second time he had seen her afraid. The last time was the day he got his draft notice from the Red Army.

That was almost exactly a year ago, he thought. *A day just like today, with snow melting into slush and turning the road to mud.*

He had to walk on the edge or the road, where the ice was a little more solid. He could see the footprints of the visitor in the slush on the way to town, until they turned onto the dirt road that led to the bridge and the road to Tesla Kuritsa's.

Today is going to be different. I've been between the vise jaws for too long. Ukraine has been in the vise jaws for too long. Germany on one side, Russia on the other, Poland on a third. It's time I pushed back.

Maurice continued into Nastasciv and reached Zazulak's house as the sun rose over the snowy fields. Maurice had avoided Hrech Zazulak since the man had asked him, at his welcome-home party, to see him about continuing to fight for Ukraine.

Zazulak opened the kitchen door after Maurice knocked just once. *Was he waiting for me?*

He nodded at Maurice and let him in, pulling a chair from the kitchen table for him.

Maurice sat. Hrech opened the stove door and stoked the coal before putting a kettle on top. He sat. "We need you to coordinate intelligence reports, code them and deliver them to a drop point."

"That sounds dangerous."

"You will be doing an important task for your country. Ukraine can be free only if we work together."

"That's not why I'm here. Someone knocked on my mother's door an hour ago, looking for Tesla Kuritsa."

"Did you see who it was?"

"No. Just a man. Alone. My mother sent him off and he went across the river."

Hrech drummed his fingers on the table, thinking until the kettle began to whistle. He made two cups of tea without saying anything else.

"Coming to the door before dawn means he's a spy," he said, putting the cups on the table. "And if I didn't know about him, it means he's working for the Soviets.

That old communist bastard Kuritsa is working with the Reds. You know how the Reds operate, don't you?"

"I served in the Red Army for six months."

Hrech nodded. "Good. You'll be perfect for intelligence."

Maurice shook his head. "You have to keep my family safe. No one comes to my mother's door in the middle of the night ever again."

Hrech stood again and went to the corner of the kitchen, where he pried a floorboard up. He reached into the space below and brought out a small cloth bag. He carefully replaced the floorboard and Maurice could not see any sign of the hiding place from where he sat.

Hrech took a German-issue pistol, a Luger, from the bag and put it on the table in front of Maurice. "This is for you. You're in the Ukrainian Insurgent Army now. I will be your only contact, the only name you know in the army. Everyone else will know you as…" he looked up, thinking. "Zorenko."

"Little star?"

"Only use it when necessary."

Maurice made himself not look at the pistol. "And my mother?"

"You want her protected? We'll protect her." He pushed the gun toward Maurice. "I'll contact you when we need you."

"What about the man who came to my door?"

"We'll take care of him."

"Don't harm Kuritsa."

Hrech looked Maurice directly in the eyes. "Don't concern yourself with that commie traitor. She's chosen her side, with the Russians. We're fighting for a free Ukraine."

Maurice's mouth was dry. He pushed the guilt away. *Kuritsa had chosen a side in this war. Whether I say anything or not, he put his family at risk by offering his home as a contact point for the Soviets.*

Maurice stood and slipped the gun into his pocket. He gulped down the rest of his tea and stepped to the door. He had not even taken off his jacket.

"Thank you, Maurice," Hrech said as Maurice opened the door. "You're doing a great service for your country."

Maurice felt the weight of the gun in his jacket all the way back to his mother's house.

He was out of the army and out of uniform, free of the German POW camp. But Maurice's war was far from over.

Afterword

I first learned that Maurice Bury had served in the Red Army from his daughter, Roxanne, my girlfriend at the time and now my wife. Like most parents, he liked to compare our complaints over minor inconveniences to the deprivations he suffered.

"You don't like the food in the university cafeteria? You know what I got to eat in the army? Fish head soup. Hot water with fish heads floating in it. And we ate it because that's all there was."

"When I was in college, we used to make a little extra money by cutting firewood on the weekends. *That* was hard work."

"We couldn't afford to keep the house warm in the winter when I was a student. I had a big cat who would sit on my lap and keep me warm when I studied."

He also scoffed at war movies, particularly *The Great Escape*, the story of American and British (and one Australian) airmen escaping from a Luftwaffe POW camp. "That's ridiculous," he said when the prisoners were digging tunnels."You couldn't do anything like that! The guards would shoot you if you moved!"

Comments like that, and little snippets he told us about his experiences, convinced me that his story would make a great book, even a movie.

Maurice liked to tell stories about his life in Ukraine

and his time in the army, as long as they were funny or if he could use them to counter Roxanne's and my own complaining. He was happy to tell me how the disorganized and poorly supplied the Soviets were in 1941, how whole villages would flee from a German motorcycle with side-car, how the Red Army soldiers' uniforms and boots rotted away without being replaced, and how the men could only wrap their feet in newspaper so they could continue to retreat.

But I had to press him for more details. When I asked Maurice what was his main impression of actual battle, he responded, "The noise. The incredible noise of bombs and guns and planes and tanks, all at once, all the time."

Fifty years had passed between the war and the time Maurice and I sat down to record his experiences, and a lot of details had faded from his mind—like his unit number, the last names of the men in his command, the senior commanders of his regiment. But he retained sharp, clear memories of the important parts of the story: the people who helped him, the people who opposed and threatened him.

Turning his story into a book meant tackling a number of significant challenges. The history and political shifts in eastern Europe were not only complex, they're relatively unknown in North America, even among history buffs.

Maurice died in 2003, after telling me the story but before I could clear up and confirm a number of details.

Shifting alliances

There were more than two opposing sides in Ukraine in the 1930s and 40s. Ukraine, itself, was a Soviet Socialist Republic, under the heel of Stalin's communists in Moscow. In 1933, millions of Ukrainians starved to death as a result of Stalin's enforced famine, called the Holodomor.

The part of Ukraine that Maurice and his family lived

in, Halychyna, was called Galicia and was part of Poland in 1939. The Polish government actively suppressed the Ukrainian language and culture, closing Ukrainian schools and community centres and actually banning the public use of the Ukrainian language in public. Western Ukraine declared itself an independent nation following the First World War, but the Polish-Ukrainian War in 1920 brought Halychyna back into Poland.

As if that's not complicated enough, under the 1939 Molotov-von Ribbentrop Pact, Germany and the USSR divided Poland between them. Most of Halychyna, including the areas around Lviv and Ternopyl, were incorporated into the Ukrainian Soviet Socialist Republic. Nazi Germany occupied most of western Poland, including the city where Maurice attended college.

The subject

It's my own fault that I did not get the full story before Maurice passed away in 2003. And even more that it took me another 11 years to publish the book. But they weren't wasted years. I began seriously researching the book in about 1999, and Maurice read several chapters of this book and the sequel, which will cover his experience in the Ukrainian Insurgent Army, his second term as a Red Army soldier, fighting from the Baltics to Berlin, and his journey from Berlin back home to Montreal.

The gaps had to be filled in with research: details about dates and the movements of the Soviet and German armies, their respective weapons, the numbers of men killed, wounded and captured. Maurice told me that the men he commanded in 1941 constituted an anti-tank unit, but I only realized that I had no idea what a Soviet anti-tank gun looked like in the opening of the Great Patriotic War.

Putting all that research into a book still requires some … imagination, though. Turning Maurice's odyssey into a coherent story required imagination, filling in smaller, yet important details like the colour of people's hair, what soldiers on leave looked for in a little town, and what they said to each other at crucial moments.

I hope you enjoyed the story, that it rang true and made you want to learn more about Maurice's story in part 2, *Walking Out of War.*

Acknowledgements

Thanks, first, to Maurice Bury for living this story, for surviving and giving the world a beautiful, wonderful daughter, Roxanne.

And thanks to Roxanne for putting up with my not doing anything but work on this book, and others, for such long hours, days, weeks, months and years.

Thanks also to my editor, the incomparable Rebecca Tsaros Dickson, for being tough on my writing like no one else ever has been.

Thanks to designer and fellow independent author David C. Cassidy for such a fantastic cover and for providing such valuable insight and advice in its development.

Thanks to fellow independent authors Alan McDermott, Frederick Lee Brooke and Russell Blake for beta-reading and much other support and encouragement.

And for advice, input, guidance and general support, I have to thank Samreen Ahsan, Elise Stokes, Stephen Woodfin, Rebekah Lyn, Gary Henry, Bruce Blake, Siggy Buckley, Barb Drozdowich, Rachel Thompson, Shannon Mayer, Toby Neal, Terry Tyler, Zoe Saadia, DelSheree Gladden, Mohanalakshmi Rajakumar, Seb Kirby, Kathleen Valentine and all the members of Independent Authors International and BestSelling Reads.

And thank you, readers. You're why I do this.

About the author

I am a journalist, editor and novelist based in Ottawa, Canada. After more than 20 years of writing for magazines and newspapers like *Macworld*, the *Financial Post*, *Applied Arts, the Globe and Mail* and *Graphic Arts Monthly,* I decided to publish my first writing love, fiction. I published a children's story, Sam, the Strawb Part in 2011 and donated all the proceeds to an autism charity. Later, I published a short story for grown ups that might fall into the "urban paranormal" category, called Dark Clouds.

The Bones of the Earth came out in 2012. You might call it an epic fantasy, but I prefer the term that I made up, historical magic realism.

I followed that in 2013 with *One Shade of Red*, an erotic romantic spoof of the inexplicable bestseller, *Fifty Shades of Gray.*

In between writing books and blog posts, I've also helped found an author's cooperative publishing venture, Independent Authors International, and for 2014, I am the President of author's professional association BestSelling Reads.

I've been working on *Army of Worn Soles* for, literally, decades, on and off, and I'm thrilled to be bringing it to an audience finally.

Let me know what you think, or if you have any questions. Contact me through my website, www.writtenword.ca, my blog, Written Words, and on Twitter @ScottTheWriter..

Independent Authors International

Army of Worn Soles is an Independent Authors International title.

Independent Authors International is an organization dedicated to raising the profile of professional authors not affiliated with major commercial publishers, and to upholding the highest professional standards of book editing, design, manufacturing and publishing.

Visit iauthorsi.org to see other quality titles from iAi members.

Frederick Lee Brooke

Bruce A. Blake

Haresh Daswani

Roger Eschbacher

Will Granger

Independent Authors International titles

David C. Cassidy

Will Granger

Gary Henry

Seb Kirby

Elise Stokes

Independent Authors International titles

Alan McDermott

Zoe Saadia

Terry Tyler

Benjamin X. Wretlind

Printed in Dunstable, United Kingdom

75500816R00094